The Story of MATHEMATICS

by Hy Ruchlis and Jack Engelhardt

The Story of Mathematics will go far towards solving the problem which educators are now facing. In the hands of parents and teachers, it will be of substantial assistance in making mathematics alive and real.

Here, the authors have developed a new approach to the teaching of mathematics. They begin with children and their world. Mathematics is shown to appear in the arts, the stars, microscopic plants and shells, as well as in science and industry. The basic principles are then brought out through play, using designs and cutouts.

The information is linked to algebra and arithmetic with the solution of such problems as: How much does the air on earth weigh? . . . How fast does the earth travel through space? . . . How fast must an earth satellite travel to stay in orbit?

The child will be fascinated by the parade of photographs and designs.

Hy Ruchlis is well known in educational circles as the author of the textbook Exploring Physics, as former president of the Science Federation of New York and for his contribution to the understanding of atomic energy as co-author of Atomics for the Millions, which has been translated into eight languages.

He is the author of a series of science articles for the Encyclopedia Britannica Junior.

Mr. Ruchlis is director of the Educational Materials Department of the Library of Science, and is also co-author with Don Herbert of "Mr. Wizards' Experiments in Science".

Jack Engelhardt has many years of experience in teaching mathematics to children. He is a graduate of City College, New York, and received a master's degree in mathematics from Columbia University.

the story of
MATHEMATICS

Geometry for the Young Scientist

by
HY RUCHLIS
and
JACK ENGELHARDT

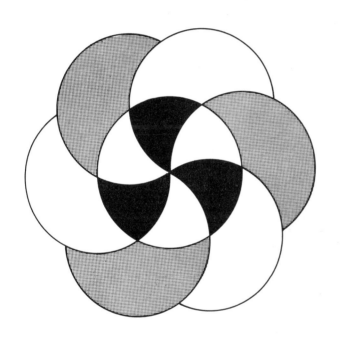

*Illustrated
with photographs
and drawings by*
FRANK ANGELINI

 HARVEY HOUSE, PUBLISHERS
IRVINGTON-ON-HUDSON, N. Y.

Manufactured in the U. S. A.

Library of Congress Catalog Card Number 58–13926

Contents

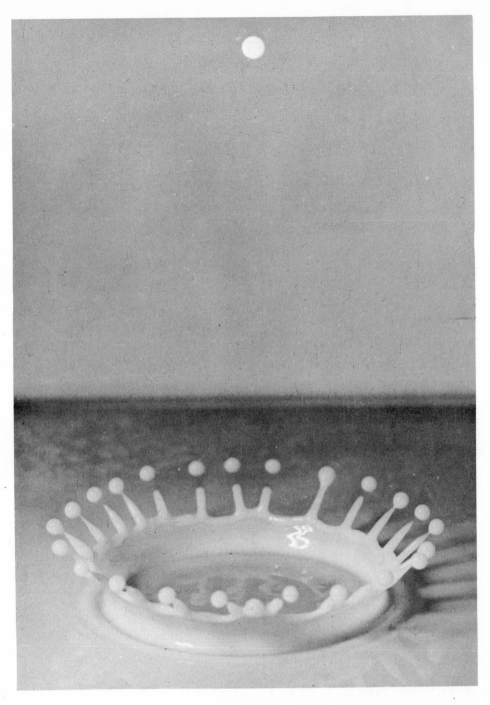

Fig. 1.   An almost perfect crown is formed by a drop of milk falling on a thin layer of milk in a flat glass plate. (Dr. Harold E. Edgerton)

1
A Mathematical World

Did you ever see a crown made of milk?

You see it in Fig. 1. It was made by a drop of milk that was allowed to fall on a thin layer of milk in a flat glass plate. Your eye would see this as just a splash. But the high speed camera reveals a crown made of milk drops, with one perfect milk sphere rising high up out of the center.

You may wonder what this has to do with a book on mathematics. But what you are seeing is nature's mathematics at work. The variety of shapes all around us give evidence of a wonderful kind of mathematical order in the universe.

For thousands of years men have been searching for the secrets that lie hidden in a falling milk drop, in the shapes of delicate sea shells (Fig. 2), in a tiny microscopic plant called a dia-

Fig. 2.   Nature shows its own mathematics in the spiral forms of these shells. (American Museum of Natural History)

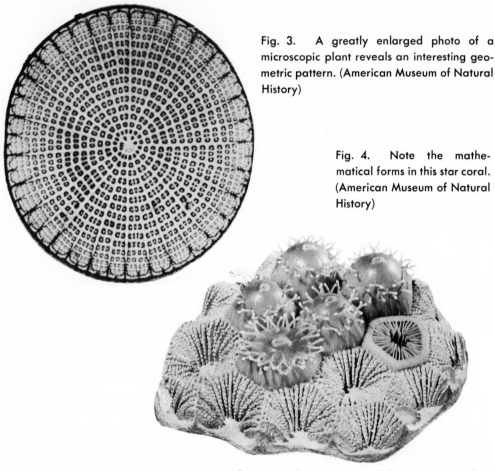

Fig. 3. A greatly enlarged photo of a microscopic plant reveals an interesting geometric pattern. (American Museum of Natural History)

Fig. 4. Note the mathematical forms in this star coral. (American Museum of Natural History)

tom (Fig. 3), in the intricate design of a star coral (Fig. 4), and in the majestic swirl of stars in an incredibly distant spiral nebula (Fig. 5).

There are mathematical principles behind these wonderful shapes. Scientists seek these principles. They express their answers in the form of laws. Frequently these laws of nature can be put to practical use to improve our everyday lives.

Sir Isaac Newton, a great scientist, used mathematics to dig out a most important secret of nature: the Law of Gravitation. He wrote it as a mathematical formula which explains the motions of the planets. Using his laws, astronomers can predict the motions of planets in the heavens centuries from now.

Fig. 5. This distant galaxy of billions of stars whirling in space form an enormous spiral. (Mount Wilson and Palomar Observatories)

You have seen Einstein's famous formula $E = MC^2$. It expresses perhaps the most important fact ever discovered about nature. It tells us that matter and energy are different forms of the same thing and that one can be changed into the other. Practical use of atomic energy came from this simple formula.

The mathematics that governs nature was not put there by our scientists. It existed throughout time, long before Einstein and Newton were born, before man appeared on earth. Today we use the wonderful tool of mathematics to open the box of nature's secrets. With this powerful tool mankind enters a new age of knowledge that promises a happy future.

Sculptors of ancient Greece studied the mathematical proportions of the human body and the forms of nature. Today, advertising art makes use of mathematical shapes to create exciting designs.

7

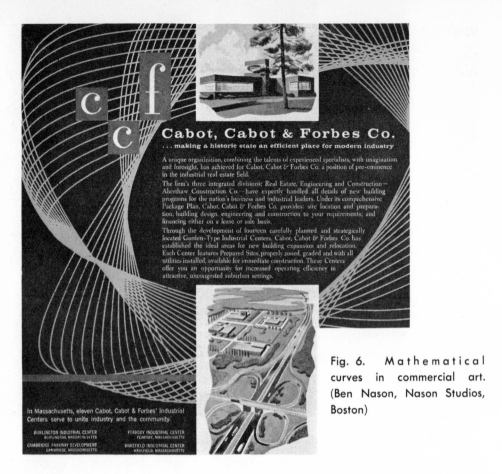

Fig. 6. Mathematical curves in commercial art. (Ben Nason, Nason Studios, Boston)

You may not know just why the advertisement in Fig. 6 catches your attention. But the unusual mathematical forms are carefully designed to attract the eye. A reader is tempted to stop turning pages and read the message printed there.

As you watch a ballet at the theater, you may not realize that a large part of your enjoyment comes from the interesting shapes and forms, and the changing patterns made by the dancers. In the photograph of such a dance (Fig. 7) note the patterns made by light and shadow, by geometrical costumes, and the symmetrical positions of the dancers. The artist who created this dance may not be a mathematician, but he certainly understands the part mathematical shapes and forms play in nature and in art.

Fig. 7.   The interplay of changing shapes and forms contributes to the beauty of this dance. (Wide World)

As you ride through the countryside or pass through a modern city, note how modern architects have borrowed from nature's mathematics to build new structures of different designs (Figs. 8 and 9). Interiors, too, are designed with a wide variety of geometrical shapes (Fig. 10). The use of mathematics is changing the appearance of our cities and more changes are coming.

Open a music book. What do you see? A mathematical language of notes to produce music. You wouldn't think much of a trumpet player in an orchestra who didn't appreciate the importance of keeping exactly in time with the other musicians.

A composer must take into account certain mathematical rules for obtaining harmony. For example, if you play any three tones on a piano you are not likely to get a pleasant sound. You

Fig. 8.   Modern buildings make extensive use of mathematical forms. (Aluminum Company of America)

must pick out three which have a proper mathematical relation with each other. One harmonious combination of three tones is the **major chord.** You hear it only when the number of vibrations per second of the tones are in the ratio of 4:5:6. This means that if the lowest tone has 400 vibrations per second, the two other notes must have 500 and 600. A composer must understand the special mathematics of music in order to build his compositions.

Now, this does not mean that if you know the mathematical rules in your field you will automatically be an expert in it. Mathematics is a **tool** that can help an artist create. A real artist knows how to use all the tools in his particular field, including mathematics, to create new things of beauty.

Fig. 9.   New kinds of building materials permit use of new shapes. (Brussels World's Fair)

Fig. 10.   Interiors are changing with the use of new structural materials. (Corning Glass Works)

11

Mathematics in Industry

You live in a mathematical world. Everything made by man —his houses, automobiles, books, clothes, TV sets, bread, water, and electricity—all require mathematics in many ways. As our civilization grows more complicated we need more and more mathematics to keep it working.

Let's look at an ordinary industrial scene (Fig. 11). There are smokestacks and storage bins, box cars and tank cars, railroad tracks and factories. The structures contain many different mathematical shapes—circles and squares, rectangles and triangles, parallel lines and curved lines, cylinders and boxes. To plan any one of these structures you must know **geometry,** the mathematics of shapes. You need **algebra,** to figure out the strength of the parts, and **arithmetic,** to get the answers from your calculations.

Fig. 11.   Many different mathematical forms can be found in a bustling industrial scene. (United States Steel Corp.)

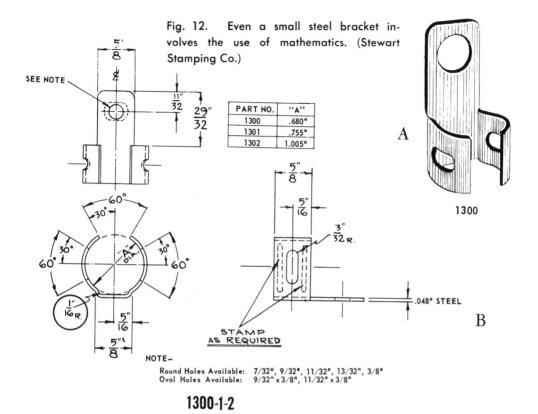

Fig. 12. Even a small steel bracket involves the use of mathematics. (Stewart Stamping Co.)

PART NO.	"A"
1300	.680"
1301	.755"
1302	1.005"

A

1300

B

.048" STEEL

STAMP AS REQUIRED

NOTE—
Round Holes Available: 7/32", 9/32", 11/32", 13/32", 3/8"
Oval Holes Available: 9/32" x 3/8", 11/32" x 3/8"

1300-1-2

The steel, wood, plastic and glass used in these structures had to be produced. Materials had to be mixed in the correct proportions. Parts had to be cut to the right sizes.

Engineers designed each part exactly and showed how all of them would fit together. Carpenters and steelworkers followed the blueprints to build each structure properly. Bookkeepers and accountants figured out how much material to buy, what it would cost, and how much money to charge for it.

Even the tiniest part in a manufactured product involves a great deal of mathematics. For example, Fig. 12A shows a simple metal bracket used to hold electrical parts in place. It might be a very small part of a radio or TV set, yet, its dimensions must be carefully planned (Fig. 12B).

13

Notice the number 1/16″ followed by an "R" in the lower left-hand corner of Fig. 12B. It means that the curve of metal, at the point indicated by the arrow, is a circle made with a "radius" of 1/16 inch.

Even this small part needed an engineer to design it and a draftsman to make a drawing. At the machine shop, the drawing was carefully copied in metal to form a stamping tool. Then the tool was put into a machine that stamped the metal and out came a metal part just as the engineer designed it.

Now, is this complicated mathematical and scientific fuss really necessary? After all, people did manage to make things for thousands of years, long before modern factories, engineers, scientists and draftsmen came upon the scene. Long ago, products were made and fitted together slowly by hand. There is a great difference between the method of production used in the past, and that used today. Now, machines produce for us. It is much faster and cheaper. We call it **mass production.**

If a modern car were to be made by the old method, each part, from the tiniest screw to the curved windshield, would have to be made and fitted by hand. A car would cost, perhaps, a million dollars! In fact, the first sample of a new car model is made in this way. Hundreds of designers, engineers and mechanics work on it. But once it is built and the sizes are set, mass production machines take over and the separate parts are made by the millions.

If the engineers have done their jobs carefully, all the parts can be fitted together quickly and easily on an assembly line. No part needs to be scraped or polished down to proper size. Within a few hours, mechanics can put together the thousands of manufactured parts that go into a modern car.

When a fuel pump or carburetor in an engine needs replacement, you can order a new one, and know that when it arrives it will fit perfectly and do the same job.

Without the production of parts that match each other precisely, our high standard of living and short working hours would be impossible. But modern living would also be impossible without mathematics to make sure that all parts are exactly the same.

Everywhere you go you meet mathematics, in one form or another. Sometimes it is hidden and will be difficult for you to see. Sometimes it is quite obvious. Let's look more closely at the kind of mathematical world in which we live. In our next chapter we'll start with some shapes and forms you see in the world around you.

2
The Shape of Things

Have you ever wondered how marbles are made so round? The glass for the marble is melted and dropped from the top of a tower. It forms a ball shape as it falls. By the time it reaches the bottom of the tower it is a round marble, cool and hard. The milk drops in Fig. 2 show this same spherical shape.

Spheres

A **sphere** (ball) is perhaps the simplest solid shape that one can imagine. It has no corners or edges. Every spot on the outside of a ball is exactly the same distance from the center as every other spot.

Drops of liquid are spherical in shape because electrical forces pull the loose material inward (Fig. 13A). All available space in the drop is then filled by the atoms of the liquid moving more closely together. Finally, a globe forms (Fig. 13B). The material is now in its most compact form.

You can see how this happens in the following experiment. Let several drops of oil fall onto the surface of water in a glass. Colored salad oil is excellent for this experiment. In the water, the tiny parts of oil begin to pull together to form a flat circular drop. Several drops of oil tend to join each other until one large circular drop is formed.

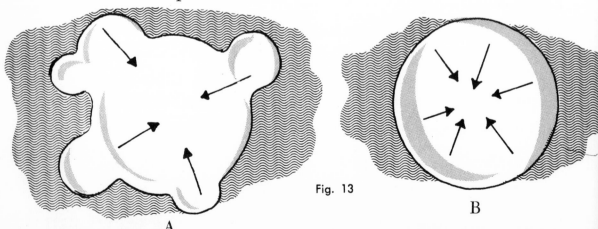

Fig. 13

A   B

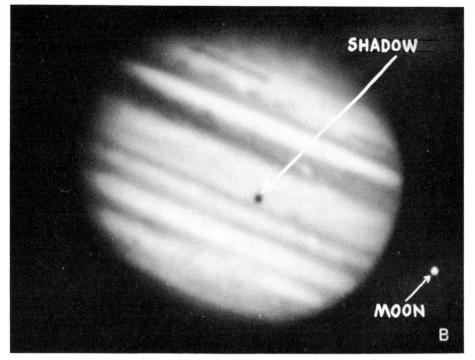

Fig. 14.   Mathematics is used by astronomers to explain the spherical shape of Jupiter, the bulge of its equator, and the circular shape of the eclipse (shadow) caused by a satellite. (Mount Wilson and Palomar Observatories)

The oil drop is flat because it can't push the water beneath it out of the way. But you can give the oil drops room to move up and down by adding alcohol to the water. Gently pour some rubbing alcohol down the sides of the glass. The oil now rests between the alcohol on top and the water below it. Now, spheres of oil form between the water and the alcohol.

Have you ever wondered why the earth, moon, planets and the sun are round (Fig. 14)? They are round because their originally loose material was pulled together in much the same manner as the oil drop was formed. The main difference is that for planets the inward force is gravity, but for drops, the force is electrical.

Of course, the matter is not quite so simple. Other forces distort planets and alter their spherical shapes. Note the flattening of the poles of Jupiter (Fig. 14). The planet whirls rapidly.

The part that travels fastest is at the equator which, therefore, tends to bulge outward. Also, note in Fig. 14 the eclipse (shadow) on Jupiter made by one of its moons. Astronomers can learn a great deal about such eclipses and the shapes of planets when they apply mathematics to their observations.

The same kind of force that pulls a planet into the globe shape also causes groups of stars to form spherical units. The **globular cluster** in Fig. 15 is actually a group of thousands of stars, far away in space. The gravitational force of one star pulls on all others in the group. The thousands of pulls cause the individual stars to stay together in a spherical form.

A ball for bouncing must be perfectly round, without corners, edges or bumps. Every time the ball hits the ground it should act in the same way, no matter which part of the ball touches the ground first. Only a sphere has a surface with every part exactly the same shape as every other part.

Fig. 15. Gravitational forces pull the thousands of stars in this globular cluster (Canes Venatici) into a spherical shape. (Mount Wilson and Palomar Observatories)

Oranges, grapefruits, apples, walnuts and many seeds have approximately spherical shapes. Part of the reason is that the sphere is the most compact shape for material. Think of it this way: The sphere has room for the most material inside with the least area of surface on the outside.

Watch a dog as it curls up in cold weather. It is trying to approach a spherical shape. By making its outer surface more like a ball, a smaller area of the dog's body is exposed to the cold.

Why are the fuel tanks in Fig. 16 spherical in shape?

Corners and edges in a structure are the weakest parts, unless they are reinforced. If a box shape contains gas or liquid under pressure, the sides tend to blow out to form a sphere. The edges are apt to split apart under the strain. But in a sphere, without corners or edges, every part is pushed out as much as any other part. The strains are equalized. A box-shaped tank would require much thicker walls. As a result, a thinner spherical tank is cheaper to make for storing liquids and gases under pressure.

Fig. 16. Spherical tanks are the most efficient for storing gases or liquids under high pressure. (Standard Oil Co. of N.J.)

Balloons are usually made spherical at high altitudes for the same reason. The gas inside presses outward and blows up the balloon into a sphere, without danger of a break-through at a weak corner.

When the bottom of the sea is explored, a spherical high pressure cabin is used. In this case, the greater pressure is outside with the water pushing against the cabin. The pressure of the water, pushing in equally from all sides, squeezes the parts of the cabin wall together.

An interesting experiment with an unbroken egg shows the great strength of round shapes. Carefully wrap your hand around an egg held over the sink. Increase the pressure evenly and try to break the egg. You will usually fail. The egg shell is extremely strong when pressure is applied equally around it. To crack the egg, it is necessary to concentrate the force on one spot by hitting it against an edge of some kind.

How can you make a sphere? It is impossible to make one by folding up a flat sheet because there are no flat parts on the sphere. But you can make a sphere by stretching flat material (like in a blown-up balloon), or by piecing small sections together (like in a basketball). But a perfect sphere cannot be made from materials that can't be stretched or pieced together. That is why maps of large areas of the earth cannot be accurately drawn on flat sheets of paper. All maps are distorted in some way.

You can make an approximate sphere by simply rolling a piece of clay in your hands. The edges and corners are smoothed down and the clay rapidly takes a spherical form.

Box Shapes

If the sphere has such a great advantage in being equally strong at all points, why aren't shipping containers made that way? Why are most of them box-shaped?

Imagine a number of spherical containers filled with boxes of cereal, packed into a truck, as shown in Fig. 17A.

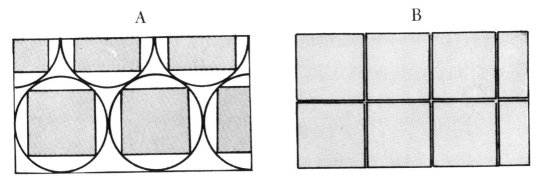

Fig. 17. Rectangular boxes make better containers for ordinary purposes than spheres.

First, note that only one spot on the bottom of each container touches the floor. All the weight rests on this small spot and the strain will tend to break the container. The corners of the boxes that touch the inside of the container are likely to be crushed. When the truck starts or stops, the round containers will roll about inside the truck. Furthermore, it is difficult to make a spherical container.

For all these reasons, the box shape is used for containers (Fig. 17B). It may not be so strong as a sphere when pressure or force is applied evenly. But the box shape is stronger when force is applied from one direction, which happens when the box rests on the floor. In addition, it is easier to make, stacks up with less waste of space, and does not roll when moved.

Why are most houses box-shaped rather than spherical? The same advantages of the box apply to a house, as well as to a container. The force of gravity pulls downward rather than in many different directions. Therefore walls should be vertical, flat, straight and strong. Materials like brick and cement can be conveniently made into such forms. Besides, more box-shaped houses can be crowded into a narrow city block than houses with other shapes. This is hardly an advantage from the point of view of comfortable living. But it is certainly a lot cheaper.

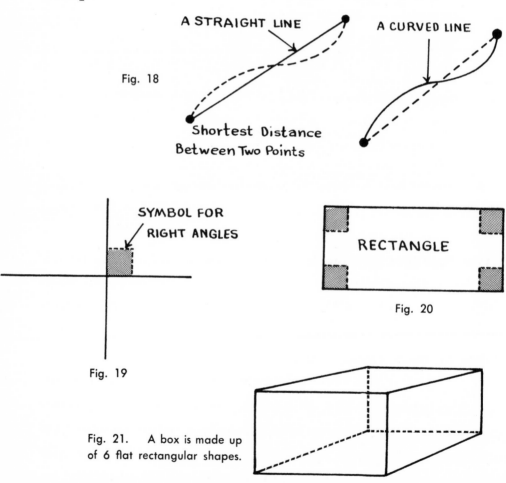

A STRAIGHT LINE A CURVED LINE

Fig. 18

Shortest Distance Between Two Points

SYMBOL FOR RIGHT ANGLES

RECTANGLE

Fig. 20

Fig. 19

Fig. 21.   A box is made up of 6 flat rectangular shapes.

Fig. 22.   Many rectangles can be seen in this building. (United States Rubber Co.)

Our materials for making furniture and buildings are based mainly on the **straight line** (Fig. 18) and the **right angle** (Fig. 19). Four straight lines set at right angles make the important flat shape known as a rectangle (Fig. 20). Six rectangles fit together to make a box (Fig. 21).

The easiest way to saw a log into boards is to use straight cuts. And fitting boards together is easier if the cuts are at right angles. As a result the rectangular shape is most common for lumber and steel beams. Bricks, too, fit together when they are box-shaped. As a result the rectangle is a basic shape found in

Fig. 23.   You can see a large number of rectangles in this office interior. (Johns-Manville Corp.)

buildings (Fig. 22). Inside our buildings, the rooms, walls, and furniture are also generally rectangular (Fig. 23).

In the past it has been difficult to make spherical or curved shapes with our rectangular materials. However, new manufacturing methods are being developed. Plastic, metal and wood now can be shaped into parts of a sphere or cylinder without too much trouble. Today we are using round shapes for some structures and they are likely to become more common in the future. An interesting example of a building based upon

Fig. 24. The Atomium at the Brussels World's Fair is made up of spheres and cylinders.

Fig. 25.   The spherical shape of this 42 foot tent reduces its weight to a point where it can be lifted by two helicopters. (Defense Dep't Photo-Marine Corps)

the sphere and cylinder is the Atomium at the Brussels World's Fair (Fig. 24). It represents the arrangement of atoms in certain crystals. The spheres in this building are 59 feet in diameter. The entire structure is 360 feet high.

Note the hemispherical (half sphere) shape of the large tent in Fig. 25. The basic shape is made with a network of connected rods that fit all around the sphere to give it strength. This framework holds up the canvas in the center so that no poles are

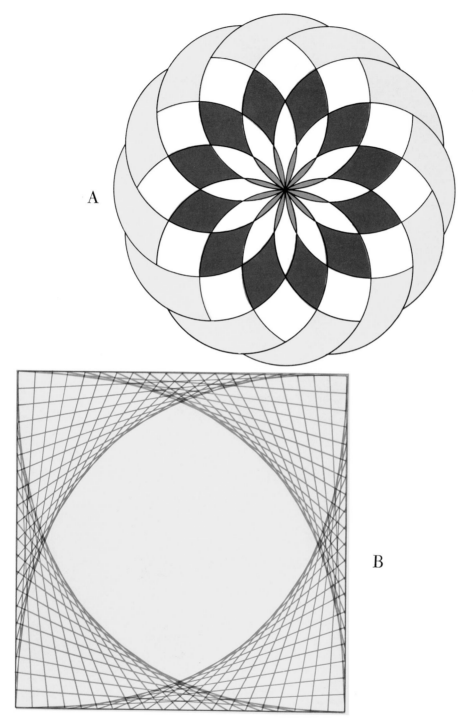

A

B

You can find out how to make these designs on Pages 82, 83, 84 and 85.

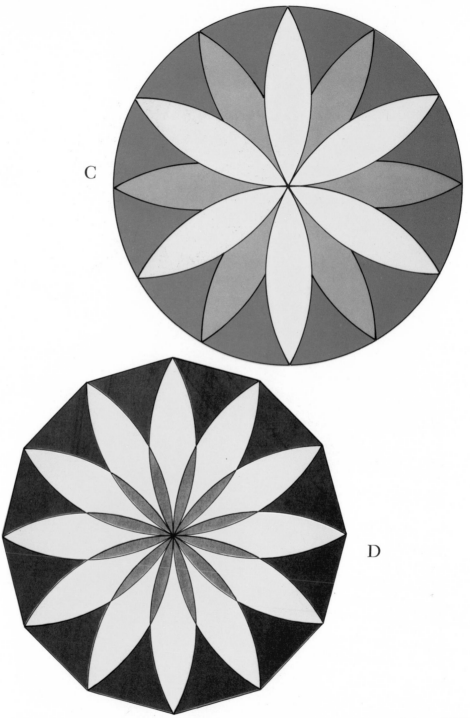

C

D

You can find out how to make these designs on Pages 82, 83, 84 and 85.

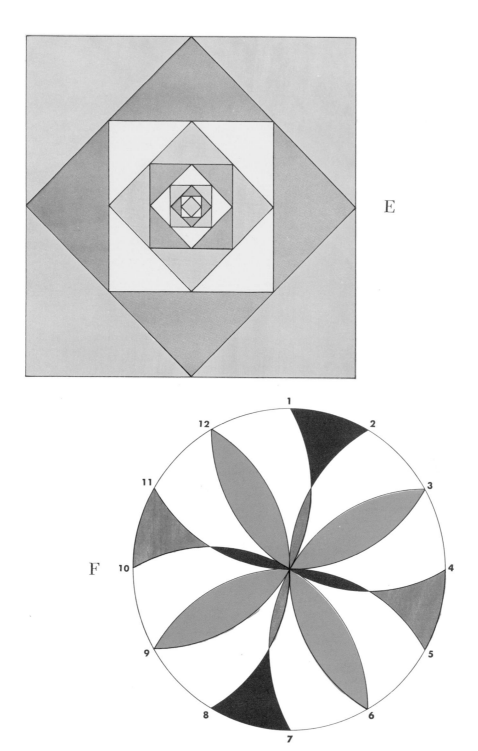

E

F

You can find out how to make these designs on Pages 82, 83, 84 and 85.

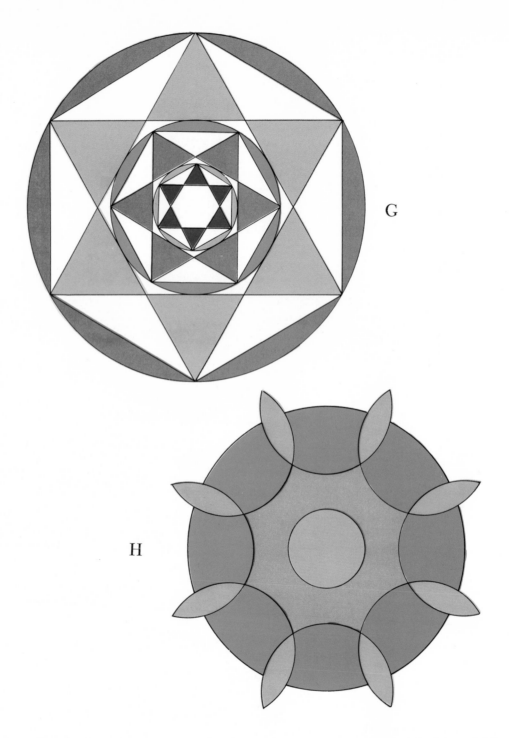

G

H

You can find out how to make these designs on Pages 82, 83, 84 and 85.

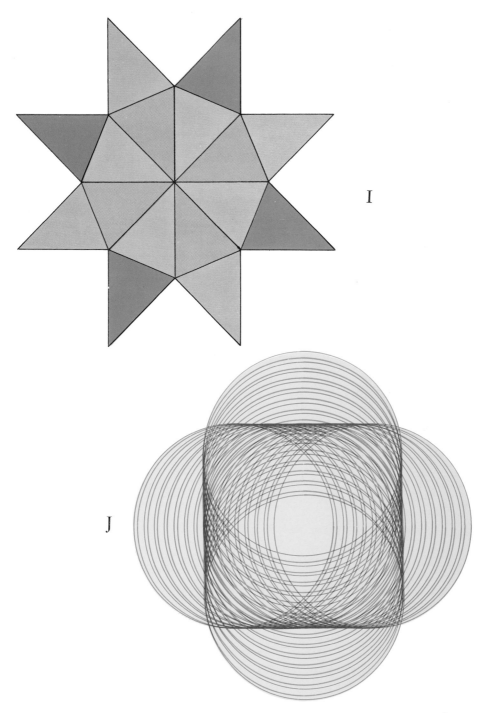

I

J

You can find out how to make these designs on Pages 82, 83, 84 and 85.

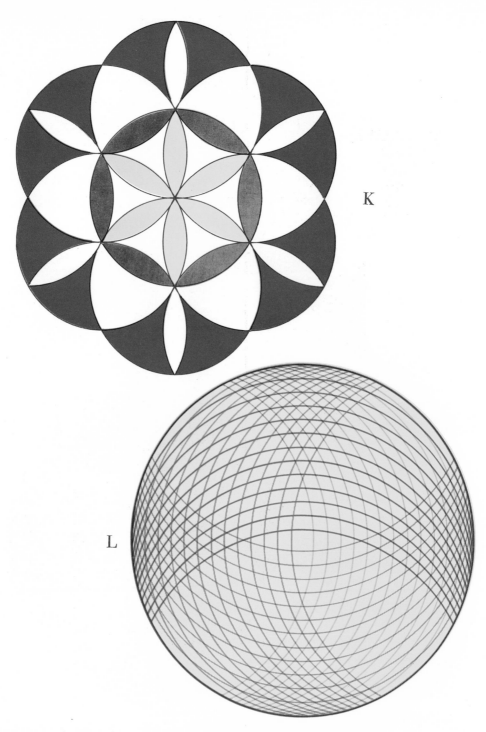

K

L

You can find out how to make these designs on Pages 82, 83, 84 and 85.

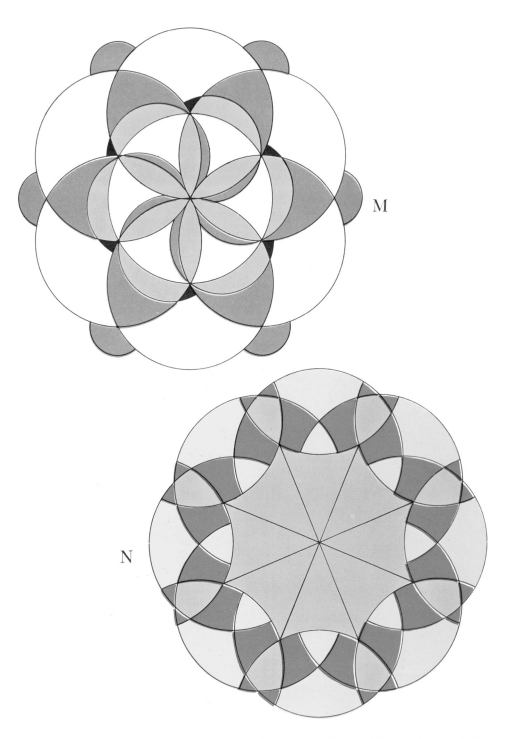

M

N

You can find out how to make these designs on Pages 82, 83, 84 and 85.

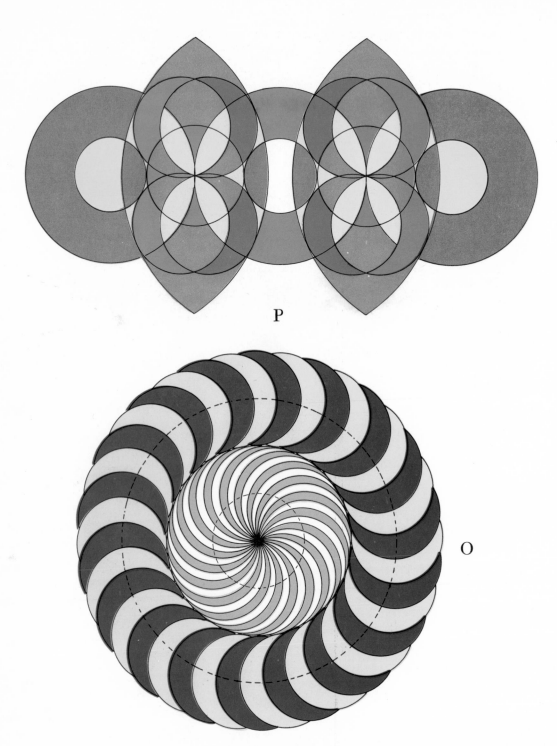

P

O

You can find out how to make these designs on Pages 82, 83, 84 and 85.

Fig. 26. The spherical roof of the United Nations Building at the Brussels World's Fair makes center supporting posts unnecessary.

needed to support the roof. Although this tent is 42 feet in diameter, it is light enough to be carried by two helicopters.

The dome shaped roof of the building shown in Fig. 26 is a portion of a sphere. The strength of the sphere makes it possible to have a large area in the center of the building without any supporting poles. It is therefore excellent for theaters and large display areas.

The Cylinder

A box shape for food cans would be excellent for stacking cans on shelves. But the box is a very poor shape for strength and economy of manufacture.

Food is usually packed in cans when boiling hot. After the can is sealed and begins to cool, a low pressure develops within the can as the steam condenses. Outside air pressure pushes against the can and then tends to weaken it at the seams.

A sphere-shaped can would be very strong. But how could we make it? And how could we stack it on shelves? So we compromise and make our cans partly flat and partly round. We use a **cylinder** shape.

Look at a food can from the side. You see a rectangle (Fig. 27A). But look at it from the top or bottom. You see a circle (Fig. 27B).

The cylinder shape is very easy to make. Simply roll up a rectangular sheet of paper to make a tube (Fig. 27D). The food can is made in the same way. A rectangular piece of metal is rolled up, and the two edges that meet are joined and sealed. Now a circular bottom is attached. The edge is strengthened by folding over the metal to give it extra thickness. After the food is poured in, a circular top seals the can completely.

Most pipes are cylindrical in shape (Fig. 28). They hold liquids and gases well because of this circular shape. And pipes can be made in long sections to conduct fluids from one place to another.

The trunk of a tree or the stem of a small plant is cylindrical in shape. The leaves of a plant need sunlight. Competition for light makes a plant get its leaves up as high as it can, above

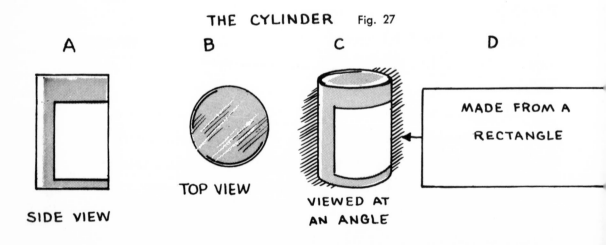

THE CYLINDER   Fig. 27

A   B   C   D

MADE FROM A

RECTANGLE

SIDE VIEW   TOP VIEW   VIEWED AT
                                 AN ANGLE

Fig. 28.   The cylinder shape is best for pipes. (United States Steel Corp.)

the tops of its neighbors. Otherwise it will die. So the tree grows straight up. Long, straight tubes inside the stem, or trunk, conduct fluid from the roots to the leaves and back.

The trunk grows thicker by developing a new ring of wood each year. The growth takes place evenly all around the outside of the trunk. As one section of wood is added to the ring of the year before, the trunk gradually becomes thicker in a circular shape. Thus the tree trunk ends up as a cylinder.

Fig. 29.   This giant cone for the top of a blast furnace is a reverse funnel. (United States Steel Corp.)

29

The Cone

Another common shape based on the circle is the **cone** (Fig. 29). A cone is a solid shape that is circular when seen from the top or bottom. But the cone looks like a triangle (three-sided figure) when viewed from the side (Fig. 30).

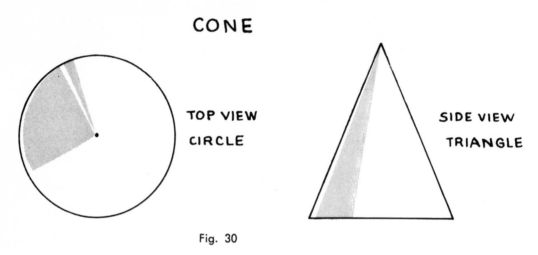

CONE

TOP VIEW
CIRCLE

SIDE VIEW
TRIANGLE

Fig. 30

You probably have eaten an ice cream cone, and sipped a soda from a cone-shaped paper cup. Have you ever noticed how neatly cone-shaped paper cups stack up? Because of their tapering triangular shape they fit snugly within each other. Hundreds of cups can be stacked in a small box.

A funnel is cone-shaped. It is widest at the top where the liquid is poured in. Because of its tapering shape, the flow of liquid narrows down as it gets through the small end and pours into a small-necked bottle.

The large steel cone in Fig. 29 is a "reverse funnel" with a closed top. It is placed inside the top of a large blast furnace that makes iron. When raw materials are poured in at the top of the furnace, they slide down the outside of the cone and thus spread apart. In this way the material scatters inside the furnace rather than piling up in one place.

It is not too difficult to make a cone out of paper. You need a pencil with a sharp point, a **compass** to make a circle, and a **ruler** to make a straight line. You may be an expert at making these basic figures. But in case you are not, here are a few instructions for drawing them.

Suppose you want to draw a line between the points (dots) A and B in Fig. 31. Put the point of your pencil on A. Slide the ruler against the tip of the pencil at A and then swing the free end of the ruler around until it lines up with point B. Spread your fingers on the ruler and press down firmly to keep the ruler from shifting. Then draw the line AB.

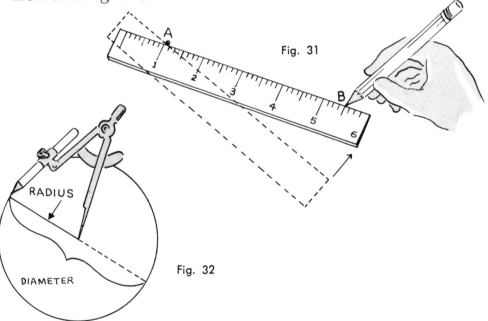

Fig. 31

Fig. 32

RADIUS

DIAMETER

You can draw a circle with a compass. A compass has two pivoted arms (Fig. 32). One arm has a pencil at the end. The other end has a sharp point.

The distance from the center of the circle to its outside line is the **radius.** The distance across the circle at its widest part is called the **diameter.** The diameter is twice as long as the radius. The distance around the outside of a circle is called the **circumference.**

Suppose you want to draw a circle with a diameter of 4 inches (4″). The radius is half of that, or 2″. Adjust the distance between the pencil and the sharp point of your compass until it is 2″, measured with a ruler. Place the sharp point on the paper and press down a bit to make a slight dent. Keep the sharp point in this dent. Twirl the top of the compass between the thumb and forefinger so that the pencil point swings and draws a complete circle on the paper.

Now you are ready to make the cone. Draw an **arc** (part of a circle), shown in Fig. 33. From the center (A) draw any two lines (AB and AC) that cross the arc. Cut out the pie-shaped piece and roll it up, as shown in Fig. 33. The tip of the cone forms at A, and B and C overlap a bit. Use gummed tape to keep the cone in position.

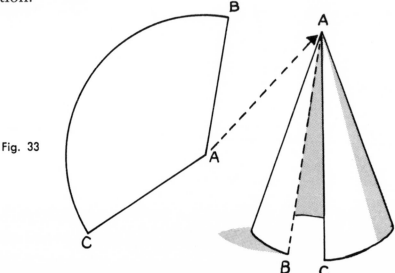

Fig. 33

Many drinking glasses have tops that are wider than the bottoms. They resemble cylinders, yet they seem to narrow down at one end as cones do. Actually these glasses are cones with the narrow parts cut off. Think of the sides of the glass extending beyond the bottom to meet at a point (A in Fig. 34). The glass is simply the wide part of the cone. Glasses with slanting shapes are easier to make than the straight ones because they slide out of molds more readily. Also, when the tops are wider than the bottoms, glasses can be stacked to take up less room.

To make a cut-off cone draw two circular arcs, each with the same center (A) but with a different radius (Fig. 35). Draw two straight lines (AB and AC) from the center, cutting both arcs. Then cut along the dark lines shown in Fig. 35. Roll it up to form the cut-off cone. When placed on a table on its wide side it resembles a lampshade.

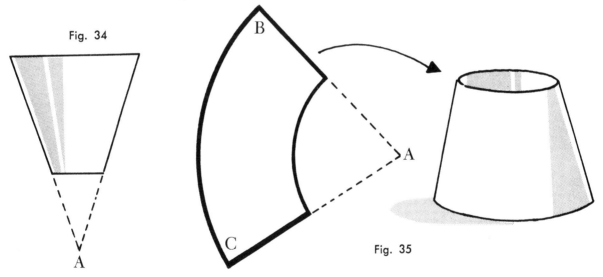

Fig. 34

Fig. 35

You can see that shapes play a very important part in our modern civilization. In the next chapter, we shall turn our attention to some flat shapes we often see about us.

3
Making Flat Shapes

Angles

Let's try making a figure with two lines. Draw one line (AB in Fig. 36). Then draw another line to cross it (CD). These two lines form four **angles.** Two of them are small and two are large.

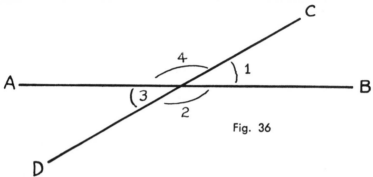

Fig. 36

Suppose we change the angle between the lines until 4 equal angles are produced, shown in Fig. 19. We already know that these are called **right angles.** We say that these angles have **90 degrees,** usually written as 90°. Two lines at right angles to each other are also said to be **perpendicular.**

The right angle is the most common one used in buildings. **Vertical** walls are always made at right angles (perpendicular) to **horizontal** floors (Fig. 37A). Horizontal shelves, tables and desks are usually held up by vertical supports which are, therefore, perpendicular to the horizontal surfaces.

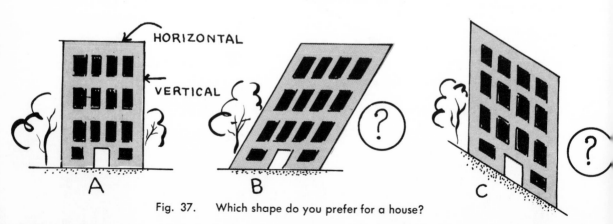

Fig. 37.   Which shape do you prefer for a house?

There are practical reasons for making things in this way. For example, the building in Fig. 37B does not have vertical walls. It is very weak and likely to crack or topple over. On the other hand, a building made with vertical walls but with floors that are not horizontal (Fig. 37C) would be a very uncomfortable place in which to live. People would roll out of beds and fall off chairs. Soup would tend to spill out of plates. You see that it is important to build doors, windows, walls, tables, chairs and cabinets with right angle forms.

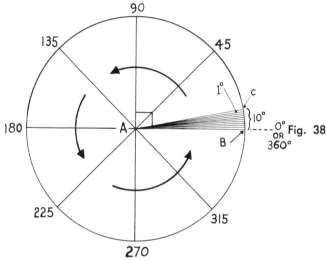

Fig. 38

You may have wondered why the figure "90" was selected as the number of degrees in a right angle. Think of an angle as starting from the center of a circle (A in Fig. 38). Imagine the circle sliced into 360 equal parts, like very thin slices of pie. Each slice is called one **degree** (written: 1°). Ten of these thin slices are shown in Fig. 38 between the lines AB and AC. The angle BAC (between lines AB and AC) measures 10 degrees (10°). Imagine the line AB moving like a clock hand going the wrong way. It is going around the circle in the direction of the arrow. The angle (BAC) would enlarge and become a right angle at position D (angle BAD). At that point the line has gone 1/4 of the way around the circle. The number of degrees it has traveled is 1/4 of 360°, or 90°. That's why a right angle has 90°.

When the line reaches halfway around the circle, the number of degrees is 180. At 3/4 of the way around, the number of degrees would be 3/4 of 360° or 270°. When a complete turn has been made, the line is back to the starting point and the line AB has traveled a full 360°.

It is thought that the number 360 was chosen in ancient times because there are about 360 days in a year. It is also interesting to note that 360 is divisible by 2, 3, 4, 5, 6, 8, 9, 10 and 12. Thus 360 can be divided into small parts more easily than most numbers.

Measuring Angles

Angles are measured with an instrument called a **protractor** (Fig. 39). It is a half circle marked off into 180°.

To measure an angle (ABC) place the center of the straight part of the protractor at the point where the angle starts. Line up the 0° mark of the protractor with one side of the angle. Read off the number of degrees where the other line crosses the circular part of the protractor. In Fig. 39 the angle measures 70°.

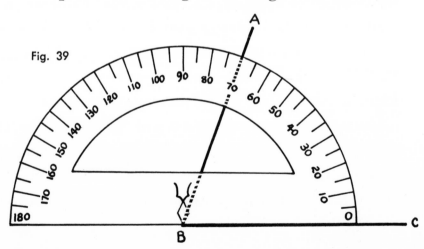

Fig. 39

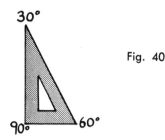
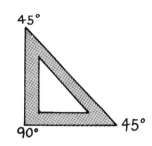

Fig. 40

Most protractors have 2 rows of figures—one row reading from left to right, and the other reading from right to left. Only one set of numbers is shown in Fig. 39.

An angle is named by 3 letters. The middle letter locates the place where the 2 lines of the angle meet. For example, in Fig. 39 we read the angle as ABC or CBA.

Certain angles are used so often that draftsmen and engineers have special triangles to copy these angles quickly. The 30-60-90 triangle and the 45-45-90 triangle are generally used (Fig. 40).

How to Make a Right Angle

An easy way to make a right angle is to copy the angle from the corner of a card or any other rectangular object. You can also copy it from a 30-60-90 or 45-45-90 triangle. Or, you can use a protractor to mark off a 90° angle.

Sometimes it is necessary to make a right angle quickly without these devices. In that case you can always make a right angle by using a compass and a ruler. There are several ways of doing it.

Method 1.—Suppose you want to make a line perpendicular to AB (Fig. 41) and cut it into two parts at the same time. Adjust the distance between the steel point and pencil of the compass so that it is more than half the distance AB. With A as center

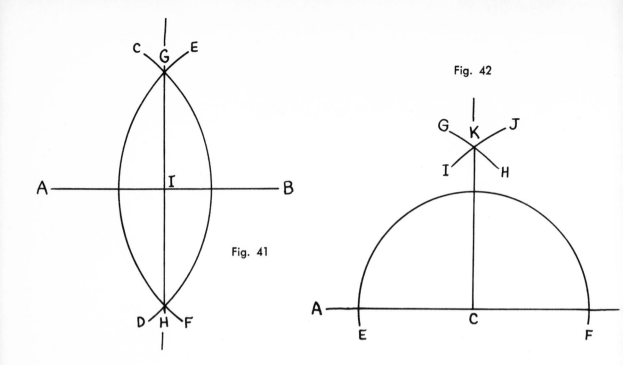

Fig. 41

Fig. 42

draw a large circular arc (CD). Use the **same** radius to draw an arc (EF) with B as a center. These two arcs meet at G and H. Draw the line GH. It is perpendicular to AB. And it also divides AB into two equal parts. Measure AI and IB and check this fact.

Dividing in half is called **bisection.** GH is therefore called the **perpendicular bisector** of AB.

In this method of making a right angle we began with a line, AB. We didn't know at the start where the perpendicular would cross the line. Now, suppose we want the perpendicular to cross the line at a certain point (C in Fig. 42). In that case we use a different method to make a perpendicular.

Method 2.—Start at point C of line AB (Fig. 42). With C as the center, use a compass to make a semi-circle of any size. The semi-circle cuts the line AB at E and F. Now set the two parts of the compass somewhat wider apart. Draw arc GH with E as center. Then draw arc IJ with F as center. These two arcs meet at K. Draw KC. This line is perpendicular to AB.

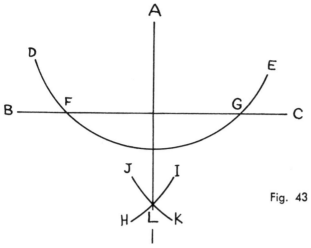

Fig. 43

Method 3.—Sometimes it is necessary to "drop a perpendicular" to a line (BC in Fig. 43) from a certain point (A). This may be done as follows: Using A as a center, draw an arc DE that cuts the line BC at the points F and G. Use F as a center to draw an arc (HI) below line BC. With the same setting of the compass, use G as a center to draw an arc (JK). If the two arcs are long enough, they meet at L. Draw AL. This line crosses BC and is perpendicular to it.

The Square

You are now ready to make a square.

A **square** (Fig. 44) is a four-sided figure with all sides equal in length and with right-angled corners. There are several methods of making a square.

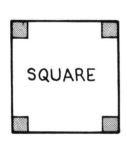

Fig. 44. In a square all sides are equal and perpendicular to each other.

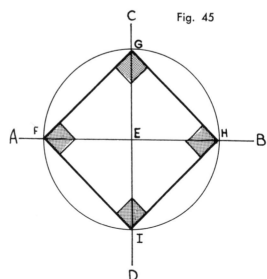

Fig. 45

39

Method 1.—Draw two lines (AB) and (CD) perpendicular to each other at E (Fig. 45). With E as a center draw a circle. It cuts the two lines at F, G, H, and I. Join these four points with lines. FGHI is a square. Measure its sides. You will find them equal. And all of its angles are right angles.

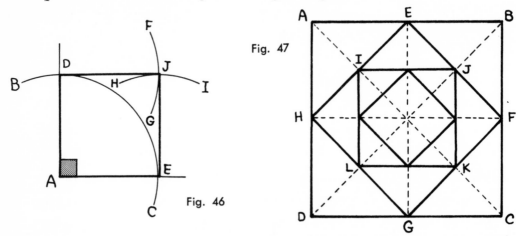

Fig. 46

Fig. 47

Method 2.—Draw a right angle at A (Fig. 46). With a compass, draw an arc (BC) that cuts the sides of the right angle at D and E. With D as a center and with the radius the same as before, make a new arc, FG. Make arc HI in the same way, using E as a center. The two arcs meet at J. Draw DJ and EJ. The figure ADJE is a square.

The design in Fig. 47 is based on squares. To make it, start by drawing a square ABCD, 4 inches long on each side. Use a ruler to mark off the **midpoints** (centers) of each side. These midpoints (E, F, G, and H) are located 2 inches from each corner. Join E, F, G and H. A square is formed. Draw the **diagonals** AC and BD (lightly). These lines locate midpoints of the square EFGH at I, J, K, L. Continue the process by joining the midpoints of each new square to make smaller and smaller squares inside the large square. Color the parts of the figure.

Equilateral Triangles

The design in Fig. 48 is based on an **equilateral** (equal-sided) triangle. Let's find out how to make the basic form and then make the design.

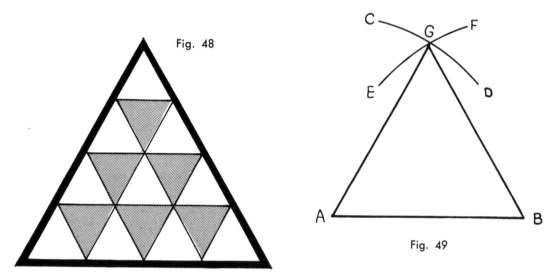

Fig. 48

Fig. 49

Suppose you want to make an equilateral triangle in which each side is 2 inches long. Start with a straight line, 2 inches long (AB in Fig. 49). Set the distance between the pencil and point of your compass equal to AB (2 inches). Use this distance as a radius, and draw an arc (CD) with A as center. Using the same radius (2 inches), but with B as center, make an arc (EF). The two arcs meet at G. Draw the lines AG and BG. The triangle ABG is equilateral. Measure the sides. Each side is equal to 2 inches. Each angle of the triangle measures 60°.

Notice that the three angles of this triangle (60-60-60) add up to 180°. The same thing is true of a 30-60-90 triangle and a 45-45-90 triangle (Fig. 40). As a matter of fact the same thing is true of all triangles—the sum of the three angles is always 180°.

41

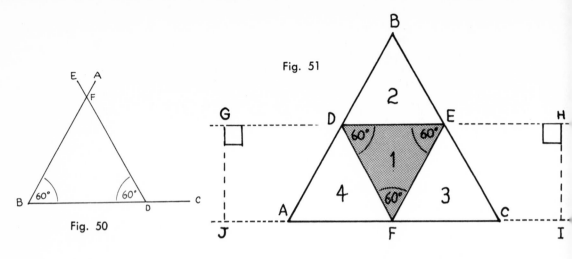

Fig. 51

Fig. 50

Another way to make an equilateral triangle is to draw an angle of 60° (angle ABC in Fig. 50) using a protractor or a 30-60-90 triangle. Then, on the line BC, make another angle, of 60° (angle BDE) at any point (D), so that the sides of the two angles cross (at F). An equilateral triangle (BFD) is formed.

Try this. Make an equilateral triangle (ABC in Fig. 51) with each side 4 inches long. Find the midpoints of each side by locating points D, E, and F, 2 inches from each corner. Draw the lines DE, EF, and FD. A new triangle (1) is formed. Measure its sides. Each side is equal to 2 inches. Each of its angles is 60°. It is an equilateral triangle with each of its sides half the length of the large one, but in an upside down position.

Now notice triangles 2, 3, and 4. They are also equilateral and the same size as triangle 1.

There is an interesting connection between lines DE and AC. Lengthen the line DE, to G and H. No matter how long you make GH and AC they will never meet. The lines GH and AC are said to be **parallel.** If you draw perpendiculars GJ and HI you will find that they are equal to each other. This means that the distance between the parallel lines GH and AC is always the same. In the same way, DF is parallel to BC. And EF is parallel to AB.

42

Now you are ready to make the design in Fig. 48.

Make an equilateral triangle 4 inches long on each side. Mark off each side at intervals of 1 inch. Join these marks with lines, as shown. A group of 16 small equilateral triangles is formed. Color them to make a design. You can make a colored border around the triangle to vary the pattern.

The Regular Hexagon

A **regular** figure is one in which all sides are equal in length and all angles have the same number of degrees. Squares and equilateral triangles are regular figures. A **regular hexagon** is a six-sided figure in which all sides and angles are equal (Fig. 52). You can make a regular hexagon like this:

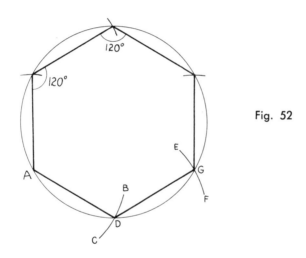

Fig. 52

Draw a circle of any radius. Keep the same distance between the point and the pencil of the compass for every step of this construction. Select any point (A) on the circumference of the circle and place the point of the compass on it. With A as center, make a small arc (BC) that cuts the circle at D. With D as a center make a new arc (EF) that cuts the circle at G. Continue this process around the circle. If you have done your work accurately, the sixth mark will be back at the starting point (A). The circle is now divided into 6 equal parts.

Connect the 6 points to form a regular hexagon. Measure the sides. You will find them equal to each other and to the radius of the circle. Measure all the angles. They are equal to 120°.

Piles of pipe or rods form a hexagonal pattern, shown in Fig. 28. Try forming this pattern with 7 pennies, shown by the circles in Fig. 53.

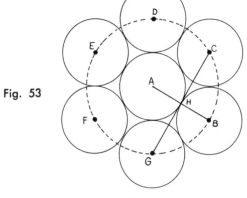

Fig. 53

You can draw this arrangement with your compass as follows: Draw a large circle (lightly) with center at A. Use the same radius and locate the points of a hexagon on this circle (B, C, D, E, F, and G). Bisect a radius (AB) and locate its midpoint (H). This is easily done by drawing CG. It bisects AB. Now draw circles with radius (AH) all around the large circle, using the points of the hexagon as centers. Then draw another circle in the center.

Snowflakes are hexagonal in pattern (Fig. 54). Every one is different, but all of them have the basic six-sided structure.

You may have noticed that tiled floors are usually made of regular hexagons or squares. The reason for this is that regular hexagons and squares fit together perfectly. They form a con-

44

Fig. 54. Snowflakes develop around the shape of a regular hexagon. (General Electric Co.)

tinuous pattern without wasted space that must be filled in with other shapes. In addition to regular hexagons and squares, equilateral triangles can also form a continuous pattern. No other regular shapes have this property. It is thought that bees make their honeycombs with hexagonal shapes because they make a continuous pattern. Fig. 55 shows such a continuous pattern of hexagons.

Fig. 55. Regular hexagons can fit together perfectly. (Corning Glass Works)

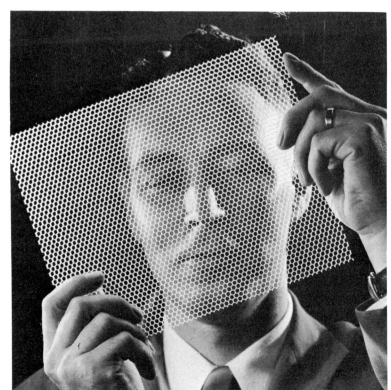

45

A regular hexagon can be divided into 3 diamond-shaped figures, each with 2 angles of 60° and 2 angles of 120° (Figs. 56 and 57). A clever designer can use this diamond shape to create new patterns.

Many interesting arrangements may be made starting with this diamond-hexagon construction. One is shown in Fig. 57. Try making other arrangements using diamond shapes cut out of cardboard.

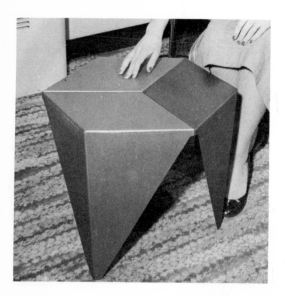

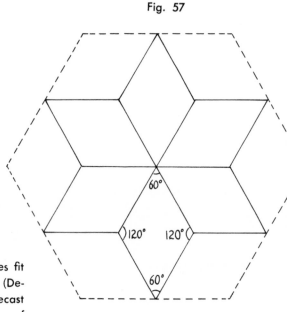

Fig. 57

Fig. 56.   These three diamond shapes fit together to make a regular hexagon. (Designed by Isamu Noguchi for the Forecast Collection of the Aluminum Company of America)

Four designs based upon the regular hexagon are shown in Fig. 58. You can make these designs and color them. Try making your own.

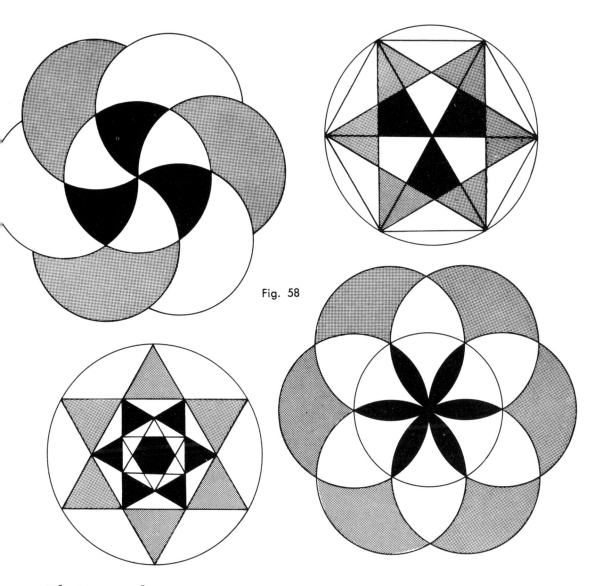

Fig. 58

The Rectangle

In Chapter 2 we noted that our buildings and furniture are based mainly on the rectangle.

Notice that the rectangle and the square are very much alike. In fact you can see that the square is a rectangle with all sides equal. In the rectangle, there are two different lengths for the sides. Two opposite sides are equal to each other (BD and EJ in Fig. 59). The other two sides (DJ and BE) are also equal to each other, but different in length from the other two sides.

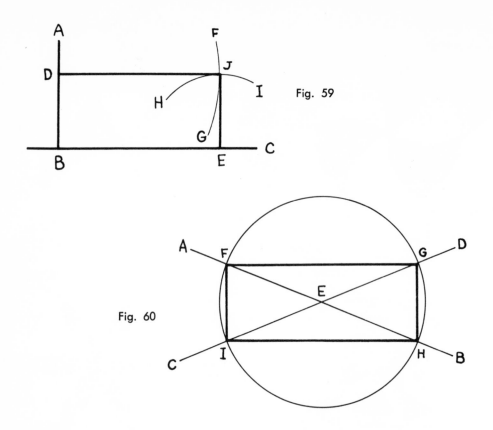

Fig. 59

Fig. 60

You can draw a rectangle like this:

Method 1.—Start with a right angle (ABC in Fig. 59). On one side of the angle mark off the desired length (BD) of the rectangle. Mark off the other desired length (BE) on the other side of the angle. With D as a center, mark off an arc (FG) equal in length to BE. With E as a center, mark off an arc (HI) equal in length to BD. The arcs meet in J. Draw JD and JE. The figure BDJE is a rectangle.

In this construction you can use a triangle or protractor instead of the compass. Draw DJ (in Fig. 59) perpendicular to AB, and EJ perpendicular to BC. A rectangle is formed because all the angles are right angles.

Method 2.—Another simple way to make a rectangle is to draw any two lines crossing each other (AB and CD in Fig. 60). Then draw a circle using the point where they meet (E) as a center. Mark the points where the lines meet the circle (at F, G, H, and I). Draw FG, GH, HI and IF to complete the rectangle.

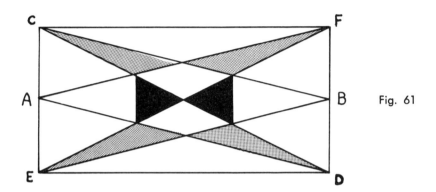

Fig. 61

For the design in Fig. 61, first make a rectangle. Then bisect 2 opposite sides, at points A and B, using a ruler or the method described on page 37. Draw lines from A and B to the opposite corners. Draw the diagonals (CD and EF) of the rectangle. Color in the areas that are formed.

The Rhombus

The diamond shape in the table in Fig. 56 is called a **rhombus.** It resembles a square in that all 4 sides are equal. But it differs from the square in that the angles are not 90°. You can make a rhombus in the following ways.

Method 1.—Make an angle other than 90° (ABC in Fig. 62). Draw an arc (DE) with B as center. Keep the same radius and make an arc (FG) with E as center. With D as center make another arc of the same radius (HI). The arcs meet at J. The figure BDJE is a rhombus.

49

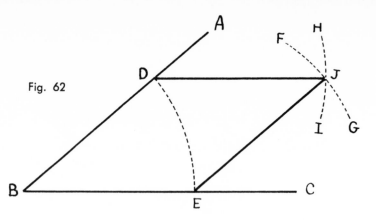

Fig. 62

Method 2.—Draw 2 lines at right angles to each other (AB and CD in Fig. 63). They meet at E. With E as center draw two circles of different size. The larger circle meets line AB at points F and G. The smaller circle meets the other line (CD) at points H and I. Draw lines FH, HG, GI and IF. These 4 lines form a rhombus.

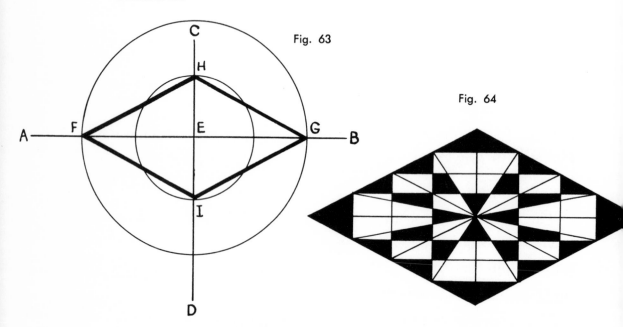

Fig. 63

Fig. 64

You can make the design shown in Fig. 64. Start with a rhombus 4 inches long on each side. Mark off 4 equal sections on each side, 1 inch apart. Then join the opposite points on the rhombus, as shown, to make the design.

Fig. 65

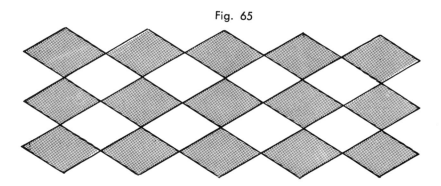

Parallel Lines

The design in Fig. 65 is based upon **parallel lines.** Here is one way to make parallel lines: Mark off equal distances along opposite sides of a rectangular sheet of paper and then draw lines connecting the points across the paper (Fig. 66).

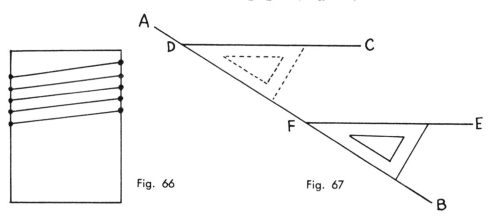

Fig. 66

Fig. 67

Another way is shown in Fig. 67. Draw a line (AB). Place any angle (triangle or card) on AB and draw line CD. Move the triangle or card to another position on line AB and draw a new line EF. Lines CD and EF are parallel. You can set any spacing and draw as many parallel lines as you wish.

To make the design in Fig. 65 draw two pairs of equally spaced parallel lines that cross each other. A series of rhombuses is formed. Color the areas to vary the design.

51

The Parallelogram

The design shown in Fig. 68 is based on the **parallelogram.**
Make a parallelogram as follows:

Draw an angle other than 90° (ABC in Fig. 69). Mark off 2
different lengths (DB and EB) on the sides of the angle. Adjust
the compass so that it is equal to BD in length. Using E as a
center, make an arc (FG) with this radius. Adjust the compass
radius to equal BE, and using D as center, draw an arc (HI). The
arcs meet at J. Draw DJ and EJ. Figure BDJE is a parallelogram.

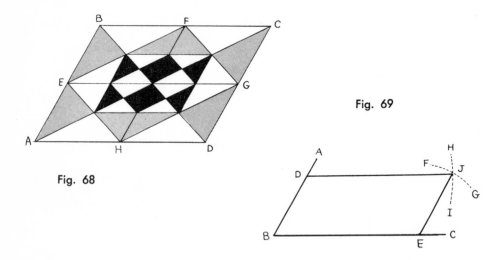

Fig. 69

Fig. 68

Notice that this method of making a parallelogram is the
same as that shown for making a rectangle, except in this case
we start with an angle other than 90°.

To make the design shown in Fig. 68 start with a parallelogram (ABCD). Find the midpoints of each side (E, F, G, H).
Connect the midpoints with lines. A small parallelogram
(EFGH) is formed inside the large one. Draw the diagonals of
the large parallelogram (AC and BD). They cut the sides of the

parallelogram EFGH at midpoints. Connect these midpoints. Continue this process to form a series of parallelograms, each inside the previous one.

The Regular Octagon

The design shown in Fig. 70 is based upon a **regular octagon,** an eight-sided figure with all sides and angles equal. The design of the eight-pointed flower in Fig. 71 is also based on a regular octagon.

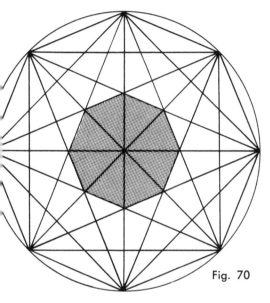

Fig. 70

Fig. 71.   The tickseed sunflower has eight radiating petals, a design based upon the regular octagon. (American Museum of Natural History)

How can you make a regular octagon?

When you divide a circle into 8 equal parts, like slices of pie, you are also locating the 8 points of a regular octagon on the circle. To do this, divide 360° (the number of degrees in a circle) into 8 equal parts. You obtain 360/8 or 45° (Fig. 72).

Begin by drawing a circle with its center at A. Then draw a diameter (BAC). Measure off 8 angles of 45° from A with a protractor or a 45-45-90 triangle. The lines of the angles cross the circle at C, D, E, F, B, G, H, and I.

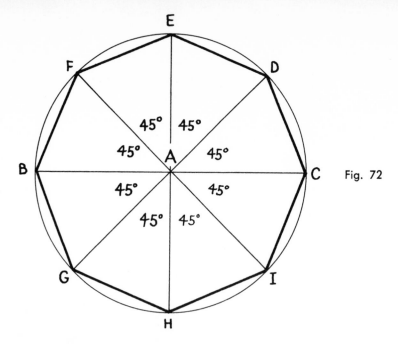

Fig. 72

Connect the points where the sides of the 8 angles meet the circle. A regular octagon is formed.

To make the design in Fig. 70 start with a regular octagon. Join every point to every other point with lines. Color the regular octagon formed in the center. You get a jewel-shaped figure.

Now try making the design in Fig. 73. On a regular octagon, join every other point around the circle. Two interlocking squares are formed. A regular octagon is also formed in the center. Continue the process with the inside octagon.

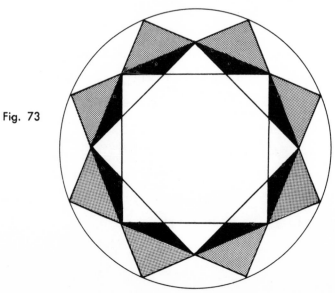

Fig. 73

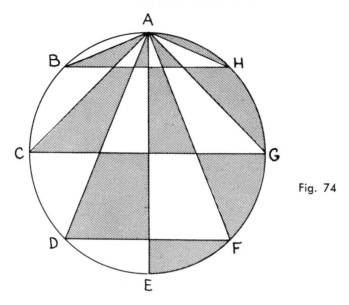

Fig. 74

Make Fig. 74 by forming the 8 points of a regular octagon on a circle. Then draw all the lines from one of the points to all other points (AB, AC, AD, AE, AF, AG, and AH). Draw the lines BH, CG, and DF. Color the areas that are formed.

Bisecting an Angle

The design shown in Fig. 75 is made by bisecting (dividing in half) the angles in a square.

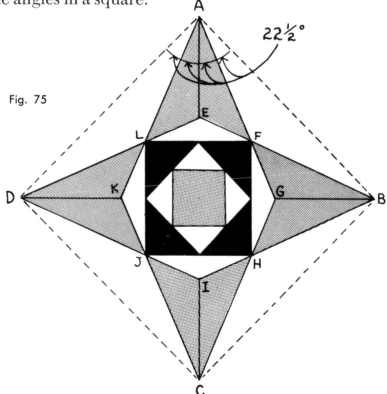

Fig. 75

22½°

55

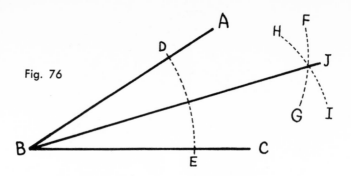

Fig. 76

To **bisect an angle** (ABC in Fig. 76) draw any arc (DE) with B as center. With D as a center, draw arc FG. Using the **same** radius, draw arc HI with E as center. The two arcs meet at J. Draw BJ. It divides the angle ABC into two equal parts.

In making the design in Fig. 75 it is a good idea to draw all construction lines lightly. Many of these lines will have to be erased later.

The design starts with a square (ABCD). Draw the diagonals of the square (AC and BD). Bisect each of the 45° angles formed by the diagonals and the sides, to get angles of 22½°. The sides of some of these 22½° angles form a regular octagon (EFGHI-JKL). Darken the lines that make the final pattern shown in Fig. 75.

Draw a series of squares or octagons inside the figure that is formed, to make any design you choose.

The Regular Pentagon

A **regular pentagon** is a figure with 5 equal sides and 5 equal angles. The star shape in Fig. 77 is based upon the regular pentagon. The construction of a regular pentagon (Fig. 78) starts by dividing the 360° of a circle into 5 equal parts. You get 360°/5, or 72°. Begin with a circle whose center is at A. Use a protractor to draw 5 equal angles of 72° each around the circle at A. Connect the 5 points where the lines of these angles meet the circle. You get a regular pentagon.

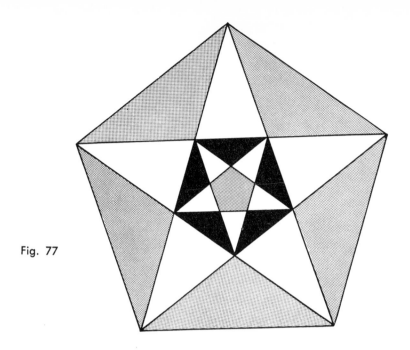

Fig. 77

The Pentagon in Washington, D.C. gets its name from its shape (Fig. 79).

Most of the common varieties of starfish have the basic pentagon shape (Fig. 80). However, note the starfish with 10 points, and one with 23 points.

To make the 5 pointed star in Fig. 77 start with a regular pentagon in a circle. Then draw lines from every point of the pentagon to every other point. A small regular pentagon is formed in the center. Repeat the process to form a smaller star at the center. Color the areas that are formed.

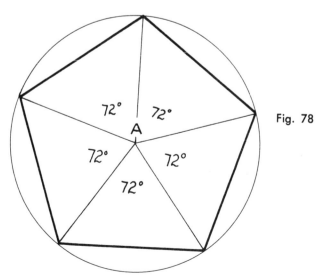

Fig. 78

Fig. 79.   The Pentagon in Washington gets its name from its shape—a regular pentagon. (Official U.S. Air Force Photo)

Fig. 80.   Most starfish shapes are based upon the regular pentagon. (American
Museum of Natural History)

58

The Regular Decagon

A decagon is a ten-sided figure. To make a **regular decagon** divide the 360° of a circle into 10 equal parts as shown in Fig. 81. You get 360/10 or 36° for each angle at the center of the circle.

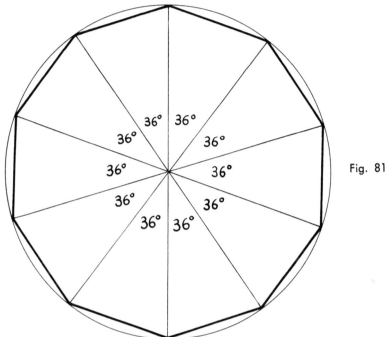

Fig. 81

Start by drawing a circle. Make 10 angles of 36° each radiating from the center. The points where the angle lines meet the circle locate the 10 points of a regular decagon. Draw the 10 sides, as shown in Fig. 81.

To make the double pentagon of Fig. 82, begin with a regular decagon (ABCDEFGHIJ). From the center (O) of the decagon, draw OA and extend it well beyond A to Z. Set your compass distance equal to AB. Now, with A as center draw an arc of radius AB, so as to cut OZ at K. With OK as a radius draw a large circle (lightly) with O as center. From O, draw lines to every point on the decagon to meet the large circle at K, L, M,

59

N, P, Q, R, S, T, and U. Draw KL and extend it on each side (the length of AB) to V and W. Do the same with LM, MN, NP, PQ, QR, RS, ST, TU, and UK.

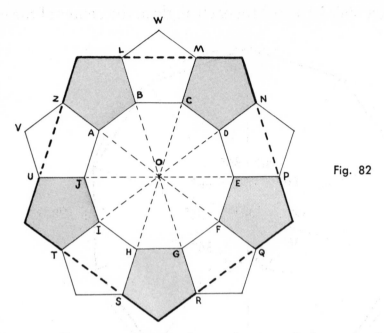

Fig. 82

Ten small pentagons are formed around the outside of the decagon. In addition, there are 2 overlapping large pentagons, shown by the dotted lines in Fig. 82. Many interesting designs may be made by connecting the various points of this figure and coloring the parts.

The Regular Dodecagon

A **regular dodecagon** is a 12-sided figure with all sides and angles equal. The unusual snowflake in Fig. 83 has this basic shape.

We note that 360° divided by 12 is 30°. Draw a circle and use a protractor to draw 12 angles of 30° each, radiating from the center (Fig. 84). Join the points where the lines meet the circle. A regular dodecagon is formed.

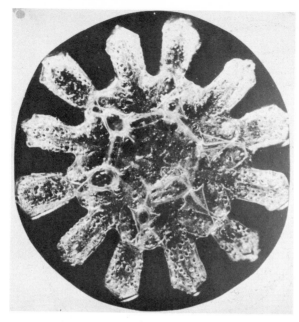

Fig. 83. An unusual snow-flake resembles the 12-sided dodecagon. Note the basic hexagon in the center, from which it was formed. (General Electric Co.)

The star-shaped design of Fig. 85 is based on a regular dodecagon. Start by drawing a circle with 12 radiating angles of 30° each, as in the regular dodecagon. Make a smaller circle inside the larger one. Connect the points from the large circle to the small one in a zigzag pattern to get the design in Fig. 85. Color the areas that are formed.

The pinwheel design in Fig. 86 is based on a regular dodecagon.

Fig. 84

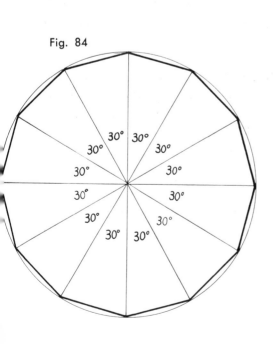

Fig. 85

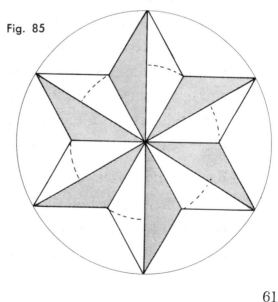

61

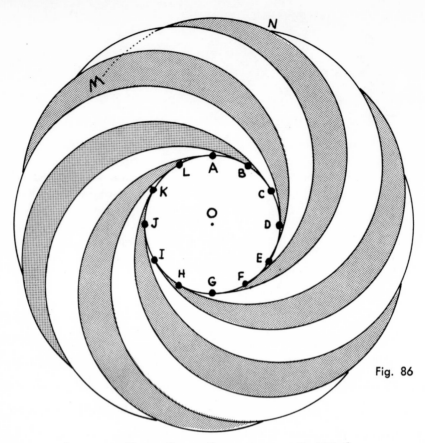

Fig. 86

First make a small circle with center at O. With a protractor divide the circumference into 12 equally spaced points (A, B, C, D, E, F, G, H, I, J, K, L). Set the compass distance to equal the diameter of the circle (AG). Using A as a center, draw a large arc (about ¾ of a circle) starting at G and ending at about M. Draw the arc lightly, since portions of the arc will later have to be erased. Now use B as a center and draw an arc, starting at H and ending at the point (N) where it meets the first arc. Continue this process all around the circle using C, D, E, F, G, H, I, J, K as centers. Color the areas that are formed.

Back to the Circle

We have described the circle and used it for many designs. However, our discussion cannot be ended without mentioning how circles are related to other shapes.

The word **polygon** refers to figures with straight sides. The pentagon, hexagon, octagon, decagon and dodecagon are polygons. The fewest number of sides for a polygon is 3 (triangle). There is no limit to the possible number of sides a polygon can have—a million, a billion or more.

Look at a dodecagon in Fig. 84 and notice how much it resembles a circle. What would happen if a regular polygon of ordinary size had a million sides? Each straight side would be so small that you wouldn't be able to see it without a special microscope!

For all practical purposes, the million-sided regular polygon could be considered a circle. In other words, you can pretend that the circle is a regular polygon with an **infinite** number of sides. The word "infinite" means a number, so huge, that it is greater than any number you can think of. Actually, there is no such number. You can get some idea of the vastness of "infinite" if you try to write down the largest possible number. Just try it. You'll see what we mean.

The **round** smokestack in Fig. 87 is made with **rectangular** bricks. A large number of bricks are set in a ring to form a circular structure—like making a regular polygon with a great many sides. The polygon is so close to being a circle that, for all practical purposes, it is a circle.

There are a great many uses for circles in our civilization. Fig. 88 shows several huge rectangular girders made for a railroad bridge. Each girder is mounted on a railroad car which rests on 8 wheels. These wonderful circles of steel rolling along a track carry the giant girders easily.

Can you imagine how difficult it would be to move massive objects if there were no wheels? Without wheels on cars, trucks,

Fig. 87. A large number of small rectangular bricks form the circular shape of this smokestack. (Corning Glass Works)

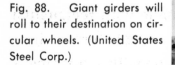

Fig. 88. Giant girders will roll to their destination on circular wheels. (United States Steel Corp.)

trains, and buses, our civilization would come to a stop. It would require too much effort to move heavy objects and our kind of life would revert to a primitive type.

The engine of every car has many circular gears that transmit their power to the wheels at the back of the car. Note the use of such circular gears and wheels in the wire-making machine in Fig. 89. You can see many kinds of circles in this picture. The wrench the mechanic is using to tighten a bolt moves in a circle.

Think of the wrench as a spoke in a turning wheel. The bolts and nuts tighten with a circular motion. The wire winds up in a circle. You will find all of these big circles duplicated in smaller form in the gears and circular motions of a wrist watch the mechanic might wear.

Even ants (Fig. 90) find that it's a circular world as they follow each other around and around, trying to find an opening to get through to the food in a circular dish.

In this chapter we have presented some of the basic shapes of our civilization. In the next chapter, we will use these shapes to make an interesting variety of special designs.

Fig. 89. Circular gears are widely used in industry. (United States Steel Corp.)

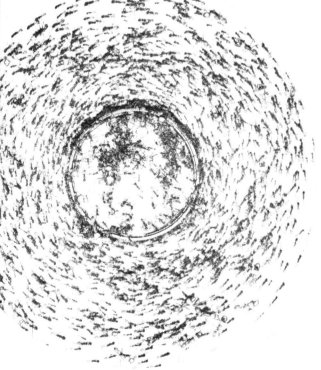

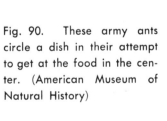

Fig. 90. These army ants circle a dish in their attempt to get at the food in the center. (American Museum of Natural History)

4

Making Complex Designs

From the designs in the previous chapter, you probably have a good idea of how any regular figure can be made. First, make a circle. Then divide the number of points you want into 360°. Your answer gives the number of degrees in each angle. From the center of the circle draw the angles and mark the points where the radiating angle lines cut across the circle. Connect these points on the circle in any pattern you choose to make an interesting design.

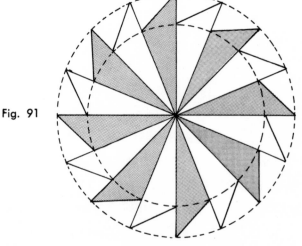

Fig. 91

For example, how would you make the design shown in Fig. 91? There are 16 evenly spaced sections. Divide 360° by 16, to get 22½° in each angle radiating from the center. (Two sections will be 45°, 4 sections will be 90°.) Use your protractor to mark off (lightly) 22½° angles all around the center of the circle. Then draw a smaller circle inside the first. Connect the points where the angle lines cross the circles. In Fig. 91 note that the lines are drawn from the smaller circle to the point on the next line of the larger circle. A sawtooth pattern develops. Color the sections.

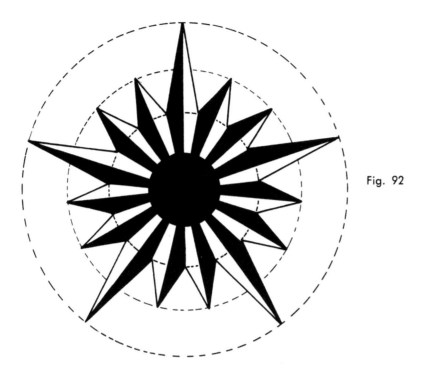

Fig. 92

The angles in Fig. 91 can also be drawn with a 45-90 triangle, and then each angle bisected to form 22½°. Once you draw the 22½° angle, you can trace or copy it from another piece of paper. You can also fold a sheet of paper 4 times to make 16 lines radiating from the center. Try it.

Fig. 92 shows a design based upon dividing a circle into 30 equal parts. There are 15 pointed rays to this star. Since there are two parts to each ray, you will need 30 evenly-spaced radiating lines. Divide 360° by 30. You get 12° for each section. Draw 4 **concentric** (with the same center) circles, each with a different radius. Locate the 30 points on the largest circle, using a protractor. Draw the 30 radiating lines from the center. Then connect the points on the circles in a zigzag pattern to get the figure. Color the parts that are formed.

You can get many designs with this method. Use your own ingenuity to make original patterns.

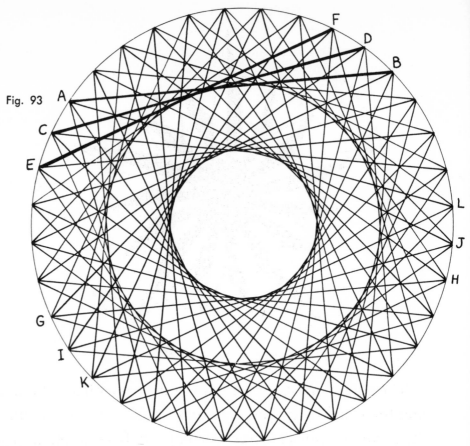

Fig. 93

Circles From Lines

You can make the pattern in Fig. 93 like this:

Mark a center for a circle on your paper. Then place the center mark of a circular protractor on this center mark of the paper. Trace the outline of a semi-circle around the outside of the protractor. Keep the protractor in position and mark off every 10°. There are 18 such marks around the half circle of your protractor.

Turn the protractor around so that it is on the bottom part of the circle. Be sure that the center of the protractor and the center of the circle remain the same. Now draw the outside half circle and mark off every 10°. You will now have 36 evenly spaced marks around a circle.

Draw a **chord** (line that cuts across the circle) connecting two of the points (A and B) on the outside of the circle. Then move to the next set of points (C and D) and connect them. You have made a new chord the same size as AB, with C **below** A, and D **above** B. Repeat this pattern with EF and so on around the circle. All the chords come together and form a small circle inside the large one. A curve formed in this way is called an **envelope.**

Draw a new chord closer to the center (GH). Draw the neighboring chord as before (IJ). Continue with KL and so on around the circle. The longer chord forms a smaller circle— another envelope.

The complex design in Fig. 94 is formed by simply drawing straight lines inside a circle. From every one of 24 evenly spaced points around a circle draw a straight line to every other point on the circle.

Fig. 94

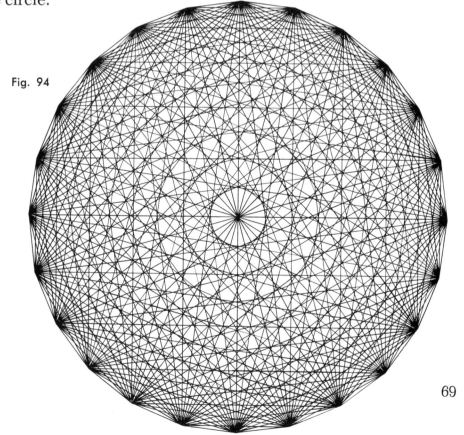

Change the design by using a different number of points around the circle. You can make the design more interesting by drawing lines with colored pencils and blocking in definite areas.

Curves From Lines

To make the curve in Fig. 95 start with a large circle. Use a protractor to divide it up into 72 parts each equal to 5°. Be sure that your pencil has a sharp point when you do this. Start at any one of the 72 points on the circle (A) and draw a short line AB to the next point on the circle (B). Now move over to B and draw BD. Start the next line at C, and draw CF. Notice that each line you draw starts one point beyond the previous starting point and ends up 2 points beyond the previous ending place. The chords increase in length until halfway around. Then they become shorter. A double curve is formed by the envelope of the chords.

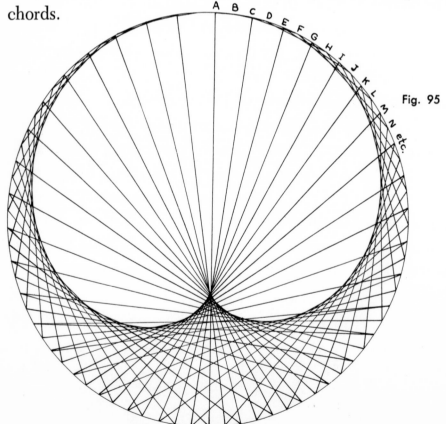

Fig. 95

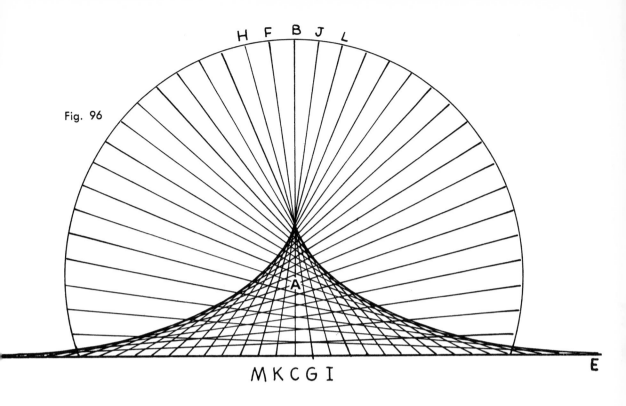

Fig. 96

The interesting design in Fig. 96 is made by drawing lines between points on a straight line and on a circle. First draw a circle with center at A. Then draw a line (BC) which passes through the center. Draw a perpendicular to BC at C. The perpendicular should cut the circle. Use a protractor to mark off 5° intervals all around the circle, starting at B. Then mark off a series of short lengths, equal to each other, along the line DE.

From B move one section to the left (to F) on the circle. Starting at C on the line DE, move one point to the right, to point G. Draw FG. Repeat and draw HI. Continue until the circle meets the line. Start at B again and repeat the process on the other side of the circle (JK, LM, etc.).

Use colored lines to give a rainbow effect. You can change the design by using various parts of the circle, different positions and spacing, and by starting off center.

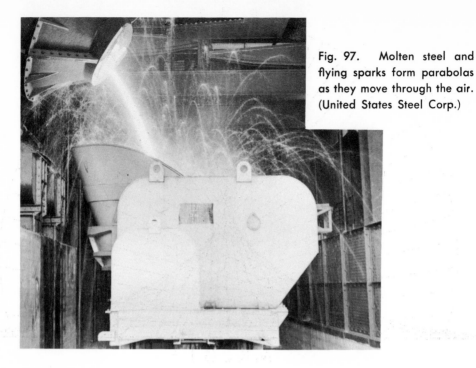

Fig. 97. Molten steel and flying sparks form parabolas as they move through the air. (United States Steel Corp.)

The Parabola

The **parabola** is a special curve that plays a very important part in our lives. For example, the path of a ball thrown from one person to another is a parabola. The molten steel pouring out of the furnace in Fig. 97 follows a parabolic path. So do all the bits of molten metal that splash and bounce upward.

The mirrors of giant telescopes are carefully shaped to a parabolic curve with an accuracy close to a millionth of an inch.

Such a mirror will reflect all light rays from a distant star to meet (focus) at a single point. If they did not focus at one point, an imperfect image would be formed.

Searchlights and radar beam antennas (Fig. 98) are given a parabolic shape to make the rays travel outward as a parallel beam, shown in Fig. 99. The strength of such a parallel beam is more concentrated at great distances. Ordinarily, rays spread apart as they travel away from the source.

72

Fig. 98. This parabolic radar antenna beams a radio wave to the moon. (Department of Defense-U.S. Army Photo)

The radar antenna in Fig. 98 sends out radio waves to the moon, to bounce back and reach all parts of the earth at practically the same instant. The returning signal is picked up by special stations tracking earth satellites and is used to set their clocks accurately. They need this information to locate the exact position of a satellite at a given moment.

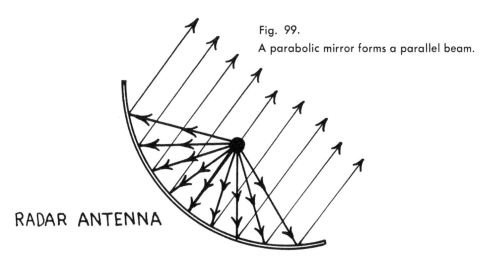

Fig. 99.
A parabolic mirror forms a parallel beam.

RADAR ANTENNA

73

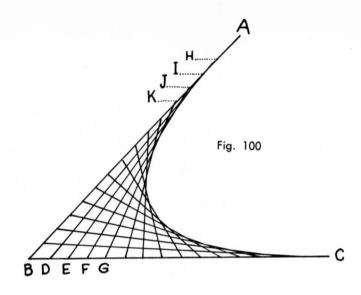

Fig. 100

One way to make a parabola is shown in Fig. 100. Start with an angle (ABC). Using a ruler, mark off the same number of equal sections on each line. Draw a line (DH) from the first point on one line to the last point on the other. Then draw the next line (EI) from the second point on one line to the next-to-last point on the other. Continue in this way with lines FJ, GK, etc. until you reach point B. The straight lines form an envelope that is a parabola.

You can change the shape of the parabola by using longer lines, different angles and larger or smaller spacing of the points.

Interesting designs may be made with this basic construction. For example Fig. 101 shows a series of such parabolas based upon the pentagon. To make this design, locate the 5 points of a regular pentagon on a large circle as described on page 56. Draw lines to the center from these points. Then make parabolas in each of the 5 sections, as described previously.

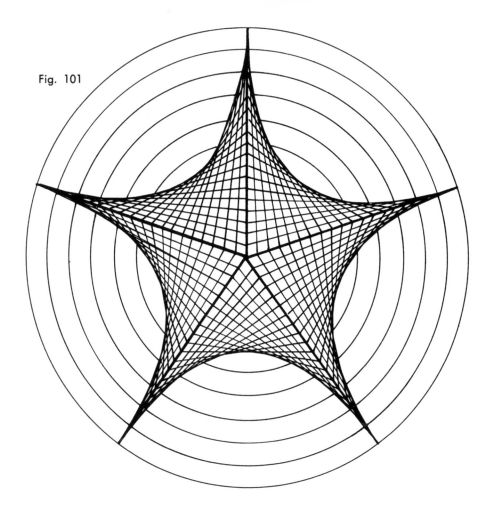

Fig. 101

You can make different designs by using 3, 4 or more sections instead of 5. Vary the design by drawing lines with different colors. Draw a series of circles and color the parts.

The Ellipse

A special curved figure called an **ellipse** is important in science and art. Orbits of planets, satellites and comets are elliptical. If you view a circle from an angle, it will look like an ellipse. Note the shapes of the pool and the top of the building in Fig. 102. They are actually circular, but appear elliptical when viewed from a side.

Fig. 102. The circular pool of the United States Exhibit at the Brussels World's Fair appears elliptical when viewed from one side. (Wide World)

To make an ellipse, place a sheet of paper on a smooth wooden board or thick cardboard. Tack the paper to the board with two thumbtacks a few inches apart, as shown in Fig. 103. Make a closed loop of string, longer than needed to fit around both tacks. Then draw the figure as shown, keeping the loop taut with the pencil while you draw. An oval is formed. It is an ellipse.

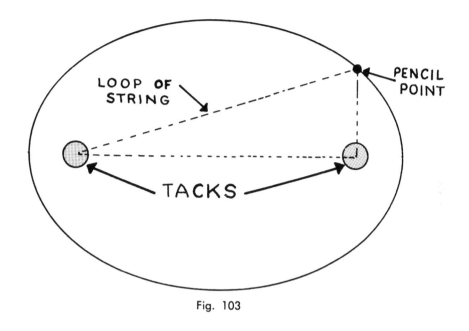

LOOP OF STRING

PENCIL POINT

TACKS

Fig. 103

If you change the positions of the thumbtacks, the shape of the ellipse changes. This is shown in the design of Fig. 104. The same size loop of string was used to make all the ellipses. One thumbtack (A) was kept in the same position all the time, but the position of the second thumbtack (B) was changed for each ellipse by moving the tack closer to A by equal steps (B, C, D, etc.).

The position of each thumbtack is called a **focus** of an ellipse. Both of them are called **foci** (pronounced FO-sy). In the orbit of an earth satellite, one focus is always at the center of the earth. In planetary motions, one focus of the elliptical orbit is at the center of the sun.

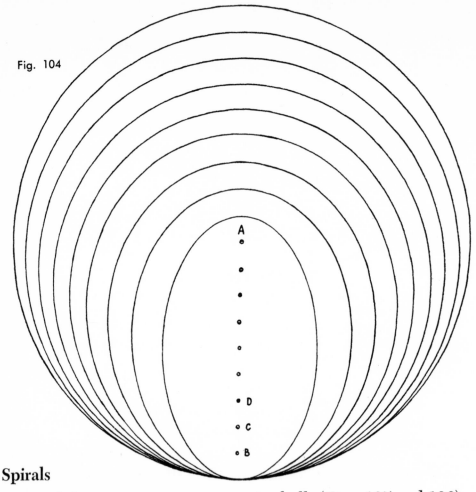

Fig. 104

A
○
○
•
○
○
○
• D
○ C
• B

Spirals

Spiral shapes are quite common in shells (Figs. 105 and 106). They are sometimes used in architecture (Fig. 107).

For the spiral shown in Fig. 108 use a protractor to make a series of radiating lines 10° apart. From the center (where all the lines meet) measure 1/16 of an inch outward and mark it on one of the lines. On the next line mark off 2/16 of an inch (1/8) from the center. Continue making marks, adding 1/16th of an inch to your previous measurement for each line. Connect all the marks to form a widening spiral.

You can vary the shape of the spiral by using different intervals for the angles and distances.

Fig. 105.   A turritella shell forms a neat cone-shaped spiral. (American Museum of Natural History)

Fig. 106.   Another kind of spiral is formed by this reverse whelk shell. (American Museum of Natural History)

Fig. 107.   A spiral form at the Brussels World's Fair (Wide World)

Another kind of spiral is shown in Fig. 109. Start with any line (AB). At B make a perpendicular to AB. Mark off a point (C) ¼″ from B. Draw AC (lightly). At C make a perpendicular to AC. Mark off D, ¼″ from C. Continue this process to form a spiral. A convenient way to make the right angles in this spiral is to use the corner of a card with the ¼″ distance marked off along one side.

The appearance of the spiral can be changed by using a different distance between points.

You can see, from the various ways of making the designs described in this chapter, that the subject is limitless. However, enough has been described to show what can be done. A number of designs in color are shown in this book. Try making these designs, following the instructions given below. Then find out what you can do with your own imagination and creative skill.

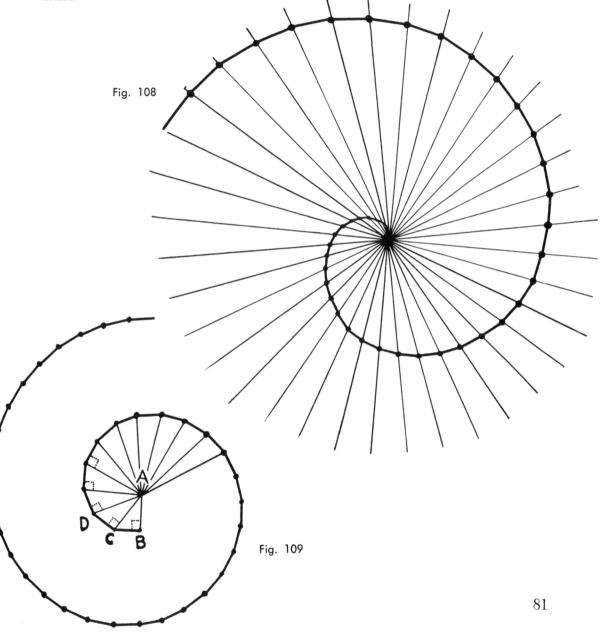

Fig. 108

Fig. 109

Descriptions for 16 Colored Drawings

Draw all lines and circles very lightly. Later, you can erase the unnecessary lines and darken the final construction that makes the design.

A   Draw a circle and divide it into 12 equal parts using the method described on page 60. Keep the same radius and draw 12 new circles, using the 12 points around the original circle as centers. Color in the areas that are formed.

B   Draw a square, 6″ on each side. Mark off ¼″ intervals all around the sides of the square. Connect these points as described on page 74 to make 4 sets of parabolas. Draw the lines in different colors to give an interesting effect.

C   Draw a circle. Locate the 12 points of a dodecagon on a circle, as described on page 60. Using these points as centers and with the same radius, draw circles from each of the 12 points.
Color the areas that are formed.

D   This figure is made in the same way as design C, except that the 12 points of the dodecagon are connected with straight lines and the areas are colored differently.

E   Draw a square 8″ on each side. Locate the midpoints of each side, 4″ from each corner. Connect these midpoints with straight lines to form a new square. Draw the diagonals of the large square. These cut the sides of the smaller square at their midpoints. Continue this process, connecting midpoints and forming smaller squares inside the larger ones. Color the areas that are formed.

F   Draw a circle and divide it into 12 parts as shown on page 60. Label the points 1, 2, 3, 4, 5, 6, 7, 8, 9, 10, 11, 12. Using the same radius, draw circles inside the original circle with the following points as centers: 1, 2; 4, 5; 7, 8; 10, 11. Color the areas that are formed.

G   Draw a circle and locate the 6 points of a hexagon. Connect the points of the hexagon with straight lines. Also, connect every other point to form two overlapping equilateral triangles. Draw a smaller circle inside the new hexagon that is formed in the center. Repeat the above process to make a series of similar reduced designs inside this smaller circle.

H   Make a large circle and locate the points of an octagon on this circle, as shown on page 53. With a reduced radius, draw 8 partial circles with centers at the 8 octagon points. Color in the areas that are formed.

I   Make an octagon, as described on page 53. The 8 points of the octagon are indicated on the figure by the letters A, B, C, D, E, F, G, and H. Draw long straight lines connecting every **other** point on the octagon (AC, BD, CE, DF, EG, FH, GA, HB). Extend these lines until they meet. Eight new triangles are formed that are mirror images of the triangles inside the octagon. Each group of two triangles forms a rhombus. The figure therefore is composed of 8 rhombuses. Color the areas that are formed.

J   Draw two lines perpendicular to, and crossing, each other. Starting at the points where the lines cross, mark off about 10 equally spaced points on each of the four sections that are produced. Use these points as centers to make a series of complete circles, all of the same radius. Vary the design by drawing circles with different colored pencils.

K   Draw a circle and divide it into 6 equal parts, using the method of making a hexagon described on page 43. Keep the radius of your compass the same, and make 6 new circles using the hexagon points as centers. These 6 outer circles will cross each other at 6 more points. Use these points as new centers to draw 6 other circles. Color the areas that are formed.

L   Draw two lines at right angles. Starting at the point where the lines cross mark off a number of equal distances on both lines. Draw a circle starting at the point where the lines cross. Use each of the points on the two crossing lines as centers to draw circles, each with the same radius. Stop each circle where it meets the first circle. Continue drawing partial circles along both lines until all arcs are completed.

M   Draw two circles with the same center, one with a radius of 1″ and the other with a radius of 1½″. Locate the points of a regular hexagon on the small circle and use these points as centers to make 6 circles each with a 1″ radius. The circle of 1½″ radius cuts these circles at 12 points. Select every other point and use them as centers for 6 new circles of 1½″ radius. Locate the points where these outer circles meet. Use these as centers for 6 circles of ½″ radius. Color the areas that are formed.

N   Draw a circle with a radius of 1½″. Locate the 8 points of an octagon on this circle, as described on page 53. Draw 8 straight lines from the centers to these points, and extend each line 1½″ beyond the circle. Using the same radius and the 8 points on the circle as centers, make 8 new circles extending outside the original one. These 8 circles cut the straight lines in 8 outer points. Use these points as centers to draw 8 more new circles. Color the areas that are formed.

O   Draw a circle 1″ in radius. Using the same center, draw another circle 3″ in radius. Use a protractor to mark off 36 lines (10° apart) that radiate from the center of the two circles. Call the points where the small circle meets the lines: 1A, 2A, 3A, etc. Call the points where the large circle meets the lines: 1B, 2B, 3B, etc. Using a 1″ radius make a series of semi-circles using 1A, 2A, 3A, etc. as centers. Do the same thing, but in the opposite direction, using points 1B, 2B, 3B, etc., as centers. Color the areas that are formed, or use differently colored circles.

P This figure shows the type of design that can be made using a compass, only. The design starts with three circles side by side. See if you can figure out how this one is made.

5

Solid Figures

Suppose you make an appointment with someone to "meet on Maple Street." You are hardly likely to meet him if Maple Street has any length at all, unless you walk up and down the street. It would be better to "meet at Maple Street and Cedar Avenue." Or the appointment might be made to "meet at 214 Maple Street."

By mentioning two streets that cross each other or by assigning a numbered position along the street, you can locate the exact spot at which to meet.

However, if the building has several floors it is necessary to add another bit of information. You now say, "Meet me in room 35 at 214 Maple Street." Notice that 3 bits of information are needed, a room number, a building number, and a street.

But you still have not supplied enough information. You go there at 3 P.M. on Monday, April 12th, and your friend goes there at 10 A.M. on Tuesday, April 13th. So, it is necessary to decide upon the **time.**

Actually, 4 quantities are often involved in making an appointment. Three facts are usually needed to locate the place of the appointment, and one more is needed for the time.

In the same way if you wish to report an event on earth, you need four facts to locate the "when and where" of the event. For example, two airplanes crash in mid-air. A complete description of the place of the accident would include the latitude, longitude, height in the air and the time it happened (Fig. 110).

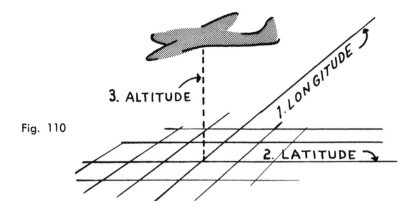

3. ALTITUDE

1. LONGITUDE

Fig. 110

2. LATITUDE

Suppose you want to buy a piece of lumber "8 feet long." The dealer does not know whether to give you a sheet of wood 8 feet long, 4 feet wide and 1 inch thick, or a strip 8 feet long, 2 inches wide and 1 inch thick. You must give him three "dimensions" in order to get lumber the right size.

The three **dimensions** you supply to identify a solid object are called **length, width,** and **thickness** (or height), shown in Fig. 111C. These three dimensions are equivalent to the latitude, longitude and altitude that locate the position of an airplane in mid-air. They are also equivalent to the three bits of information given in making an appointment "in **room 35** at **214 Maple St.**"

Suppose you are considering the area of a piece of land. In that case it is usually enough to mention 2 figures, the length and the width. Since you are concerned with the **surface** of the land, you have no need to consider its thickness, unless you are digging a mine.

A surface has only 2 dimensions (Fig. 111B). One dimension means length only—no width, no height. When traveling by car between two cities, we often talk about the distance, or length of the trip. The **line,** or road, we take has only 1 dimension—length (Fig. 111A).

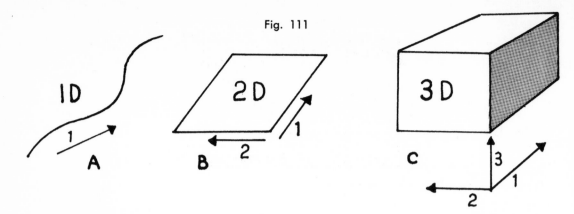

Fig. 111

You have heard the expression "3D" in regard to movies or pictures. What does it mean? Pictures on flat paper and images on screens have only 2 dimensions: length and width, but no thickness. An artist can draw a picture to give the illusion of thickness. We then say that it is 3 dimensional, or "3D." But the picture is not really 3 dimensional at all.

In "3D" movies, certain optical tricks are played to give the impressions of solidity. But you would never be able to take it in your hands and feel the supposedly "3D" picture you can see on the screen. Nor could you throw it at a target. It is nothing but "2D" masquerading as "3D." But there would be no mistaking the 3 dimensions of an apple. You can feel that it is solid. You would know that it is "3D" if anyone threw an apple at you.

In his Theory of Relativity, Einstein made a major contribution to science in tying together the 3 dimensions of space with the **fourth dimension** of time. He showed that space and time affect each other, and give us our "4D" world.

Are there 5D, 6D, or 7D in our universe? This question involves higher mathematics. If you go on with your studies, you may some day find out about such ideas. Perhaps you will make original contributions to our knowledge of this interesting subject.

In Chapter 2 we discussed several "3D" objects, such as the sphere, box, cylinder and cone. There are various other solid shapes. They are called **polyhedrons** (PAHL-ih-HEE-drunns). Many of them have flat surfaces and can be constructed from flat cardboard.

Let us start with our regular figures, like the equilateral triangle, the square, the pentagon, etc., and see which shapes we can make. Can we make regular solid shapes, using only equilateral triangles all the same size?

Solids Based on Triangles

Three such shapes are possible. The simplest consists of 4 equilateral triangles (Fig. 112.). It is called a **tetrahedron** (TETT-ruh-HEE-drunn, "tetra" means 4).

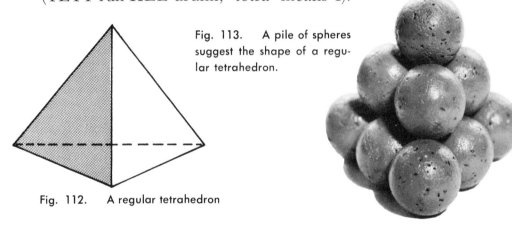

Fig. 113. A pile of spheres suggest the shape of a regular tetrahedron.

Fig. 112. A regular tetrahedron

The most compact arrangement of atoms is that of a tetrahedron. Think of atoms as small spheres. The closest they can get to each other is in the arrangement shown in Fig. 113. Note that each side of the pile of spheres is the shape of an equilateral triangle. There are 4 such sides (including the bottom). Check this fact by making such a pile of oranges, marbles or ping pong balls. If necessary, fasten the marbles or ping pong balls together temporarily with gummed tape.

There is an interesting puzzle involving the tetrahedron. Try it on your friends. Place 7 toothpicks (or matches) on a table in the position shown in Fig. 114A. Ask your friend to remove one toothpick, and then make 4 equilateral triangles out of the 6 remaining toothpicks. In other words, make one more equilateral triangle with one less toothpick. Moreover, each such triangle must be the same size as the original ones shown in Fig. 114A. When he fails, show him that his trouble is "2D" vision. He can easily solve the problem by making a "3D" tetrahedron, shown in Fig. 114B.

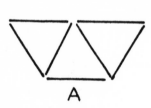
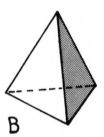

Fig. 114

How can you make a tetrahedron? Draw 4 equilateral triangles with flaps, shown in Fig. 115. Use thin, stiff cardboard material of the type used for file folders. Some magazine covers are thick enough to use. Cut along the heavy lines shown in the drawing. With a dull knife make a crease along each dotted line. This will enable you to fold the figure. Use gummed tape over the flaps to fasten the tetrahedron together.

Use the same general method of making solid shapes for all the figures that follow. First draw the figure on cardboard. Second, cut out along the heavy lines. Third, crease the dotted

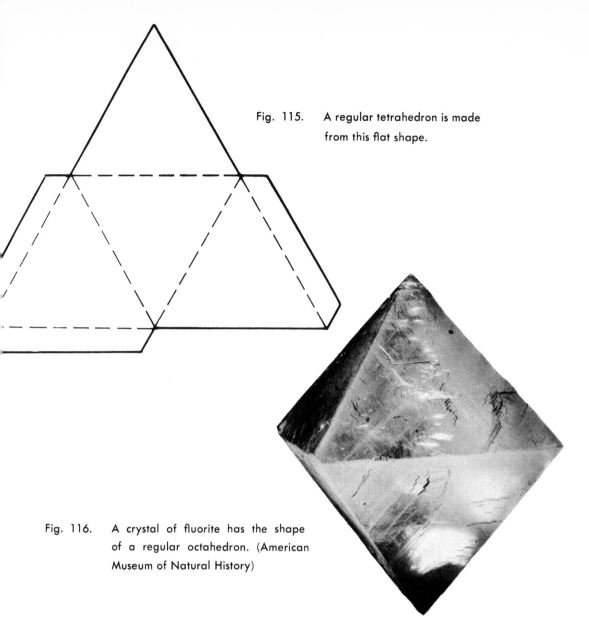

Fig. 115. A regular tetrahedron is made from this flat shape.

Fig. 116. A crystal of fluorite has the shape of a regular octahedron. (American Museum of Natural History)

lines with a dull knife. Fourth, fold up the figure and paste down the flaps.

An 8-sided regular solid made of equilateral triangles is shown in Fig. 116. It is an **octahedron** ("octa" means 8). The octahedron in Fig. 116 is a photograph of a crystal of the mineral called fluorite. Many minerals form crystals in this shape.

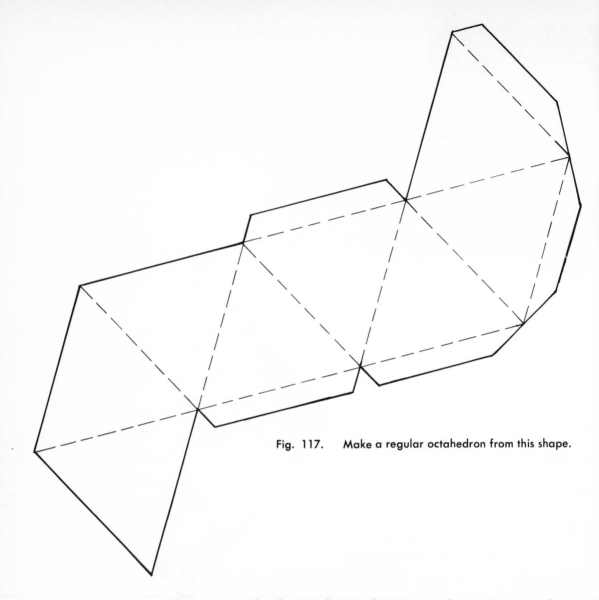

Fig. 117.   Make a regular octahedron from this shape.

To make an octahedron, draw the 8 equilateral triangles, shown in Fig. 117, on cardboard. Then crease and fold to form the 3 dimensional solid.

Another regular solid based upon equilateral triangles is the **icosahedron** (EYE-koh-suh-HEE-drunn, Fig. 118). It is composed of 20 such triangles ("icosa" means 20). Draw the equilateral triangles as shown in Fig. 119 and fold up to make this shape.

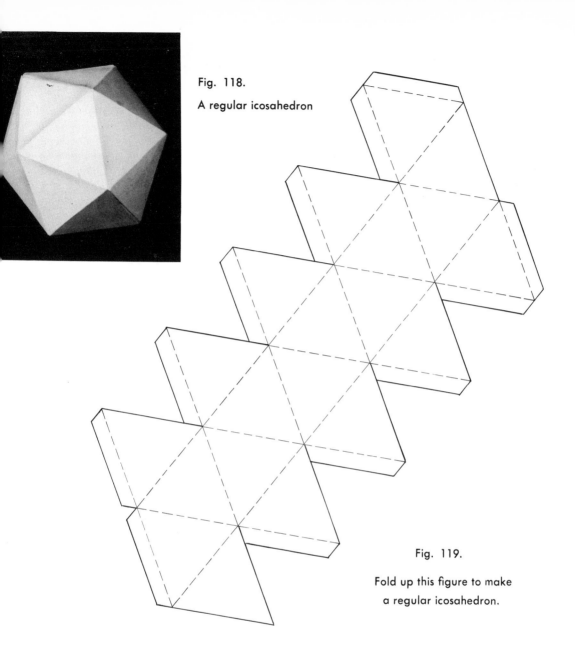

Fig. 118.

A regular icosahedron

Fig. 119.

Fold up this figure to make
a regular icosahedron.

Other Regular Solids

The regular tetrahedron, octahedron, and icosahedron are
the only regular solid forms that can be made from equilateral
triangles. Actually, there are only 5 regular solids. Every face
in a regular solid is the same regular polygon, exactly like every
other one, and with every corner the same as all others. In

Fig. 120.   A cube

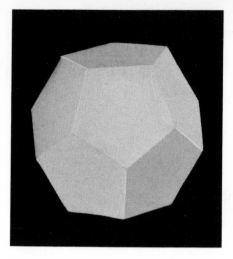

Fig. 121.   A regular dodecahedron

addition to the 3 polyhedrons (solids) that we have mentioned, there are the cube (Fig. 120), based upon squares, and the 12-sided dodecahedron (Fig. 121), based upon the regular pentagon. This completes the list of **regular** solids.

Several minerals such as gold, silver, and ordinary table salt form crystals that are cubic in shape (Fig. 122). A cardboard model of the cube can be made by drawing 6 squares plus flaps, as shown in Fig. 123, and folding up the figure.

Fig. 122.   These zeolite crystals are cubic in shape. (Union Carbide Corp.)

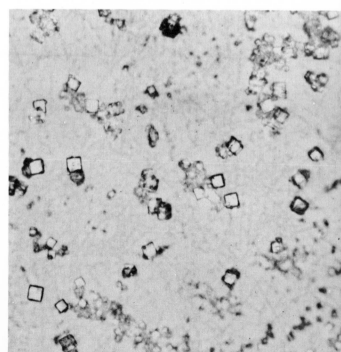

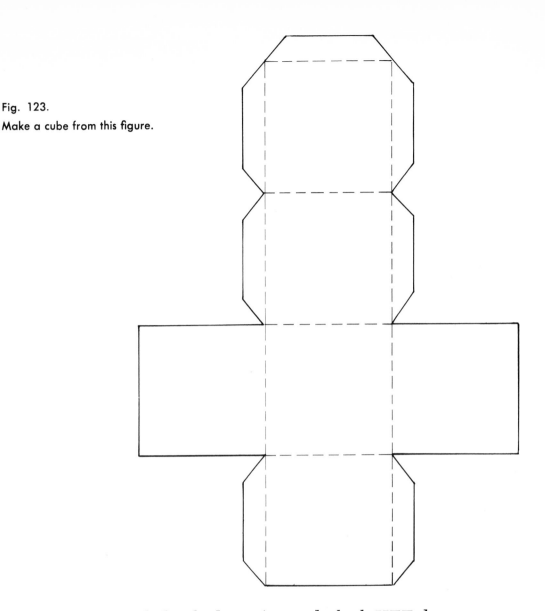

Fig. 123.
Make a cube from this figure.

The 12-sided dodecahedron (DOH-deck-uh-HEE-drunn, "dodeca" means 12) may be formed from flat cardboard by drawing 12 regular pentagons, as shown in Fig. 124 and folding up the figure. You can save time by drawing one regular pentagon accurately and then carefully tracing the others from it on paper. Paste the final drawing on cardboard and complete the figure. The final assembly of the figure will be tricky. It may be necessary to fold some flaps under, and others over the faces to make the figure come out right.

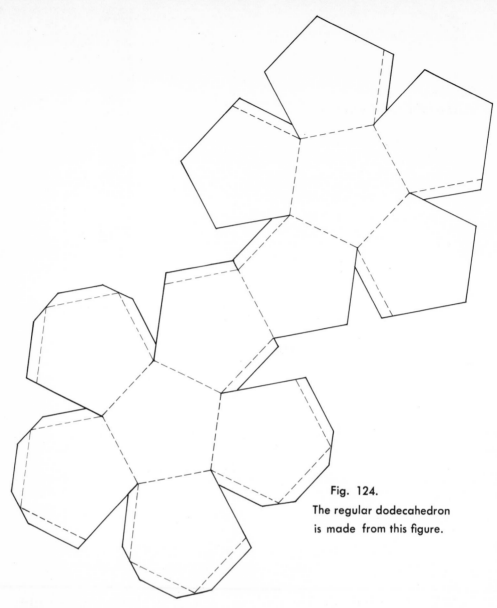

Fig. 124.
The regular dodecahedron
is made from this figure.

Prisms

Solids with flat surfaces that are not regular (not all alike) give us a wide variety of shapes to construct. For example, Figs. 125 and 126 show two kinds of **prisms.** Note that the edges running from top to bottom are parallel, and the top and bottom faces are equal and parallel to each other. Both of these prisms have sides at right angles to the base. Therefore, they are called **right prisms.**

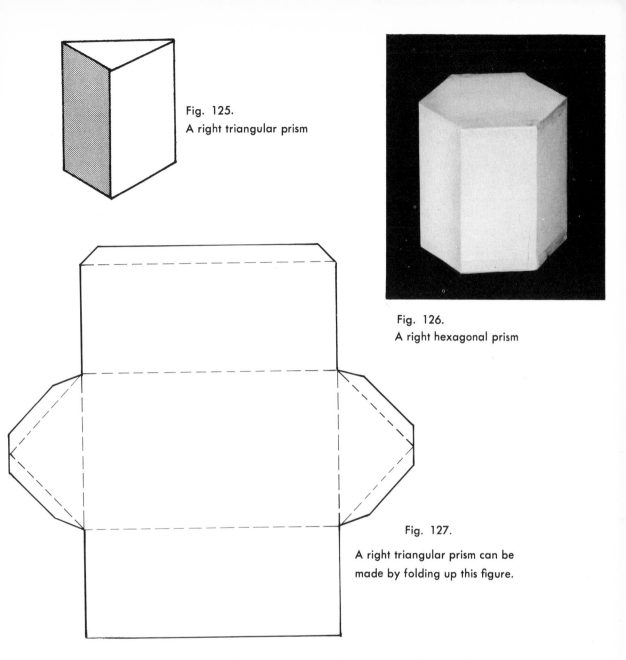

Fig. 125.
A right triangular prism

Fig. 126.
A right hexagonal prism

Fig. 127.

A right triangular prism can be made by folding up this figure.

In Fig. 125, the prism has a triangular base and its sides are at right angles to the base. It is therefore called a **right triangular prism.** A block of glass of this shape is used in an important instrument called a **spectroscope.** It breaks up white light to form a spectrum of rainbow colors. This use is so important that most people think of a prism only as a right triangular type.

You can make a right triangular prism from the drawing shown in Fig. 127. Note that there are 3 equal rectangles for the sides of the prism and 2 equal triangles, one at each end, that form the top and bottom. The triangles can be any type you choose.

The **right hexagonal prism** of Fig. 126 can be made from 6 rectangles and 2 hexagons, as shown in Fig. 128. The rectangles fold up to form the vertical sides of the prism and then the hexagons fold up to become the top and bottom. Six rectangles are needed for the 6 faces.

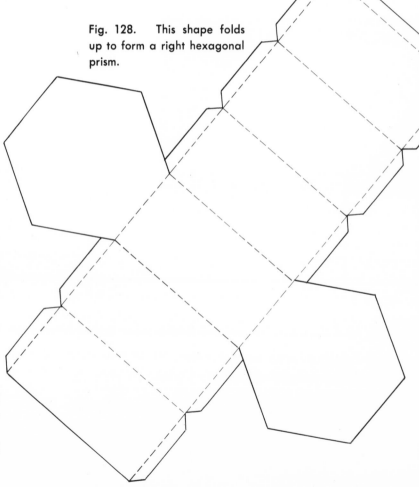

Fig. 128. This shape folds up to form a right hexagonal prism.

Fig. 129. The beryl crystal has the shape of a right hexagonal prism.
(American Museum of Natural History)

A number of crystals are formed in the shape of a hexagonal prism. The **beryl** crystal (emerald) of Fig. 129 has this basic shape, with slight differences at the top and bottom.

How would you make a **right pentagonal prism?** Use the same method as for the triangular or the hexagonal prism. Start by drawing a regular pentagon. Then draw a rectangle on one side of the pentagon. Draw another pentagon on the opposite side of the rectangle. Now draw 4 more rectangles of the same size next to the orignal one. Fold up the drawing to make the right pentagonal prism.

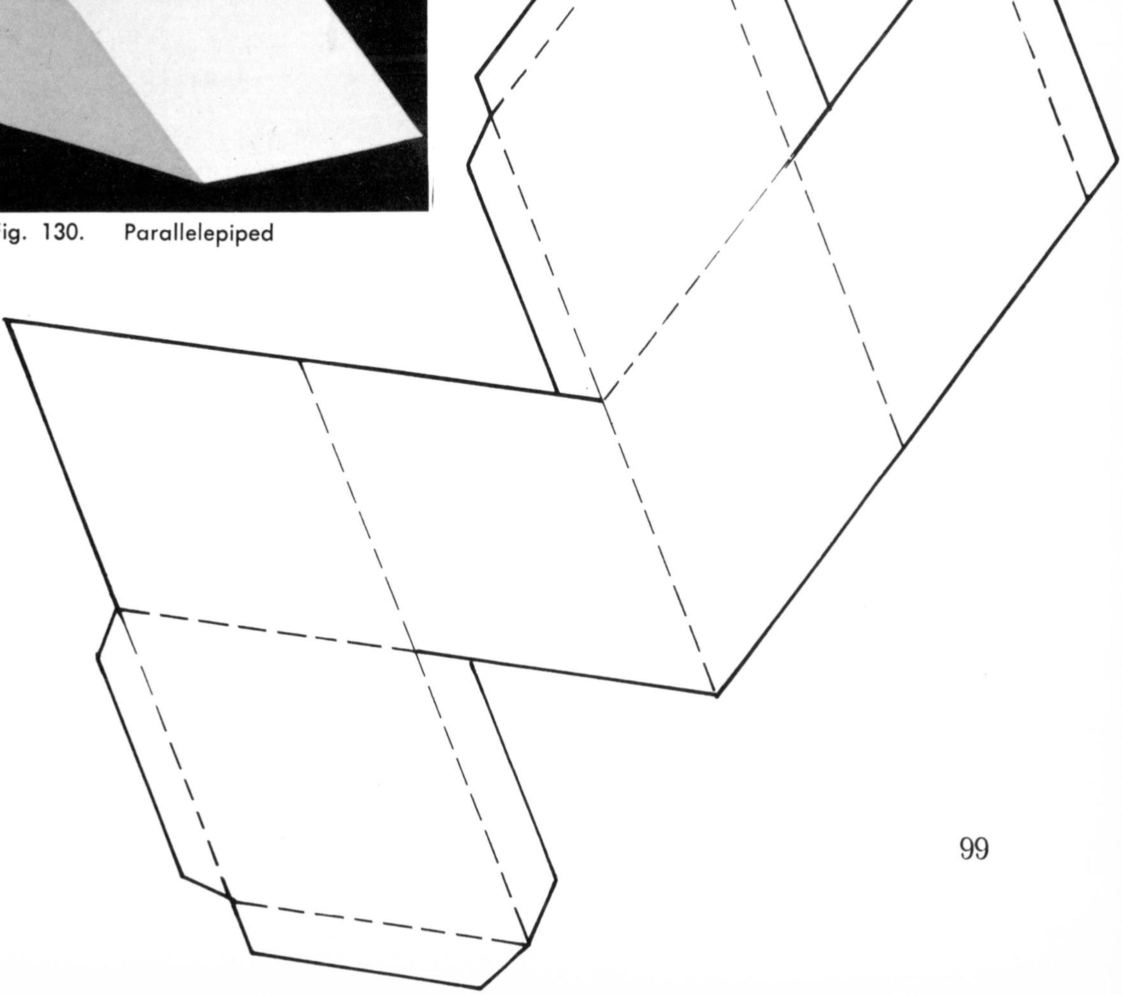

Fig. 131. This figure folds up to form a parallelepiped.

Fig. 130. Parallelepiped

99

The top and bottom need not be regular in shape. You can start with any figure at all. But the widths of the rectangles that you make will have to be adjusted to fit the shapes of the top and bottom of the figure. Try making one.

Notice that the cube in Fig. 120 is a **square prism.** It is made in the same way as other prisms. There are 4 squares to form the sides. Then 2 squares are attached to the sides for the top and bottom (Fig. 123).

The sides of a prism need not form right angles with the base. Thus the prism shown in Fig. 130 has a rhombus shape for sides and equal rhombuses for top and bottom. It is called a **parallelepiped** (PAA-ruh-LELL-eh-PIE-pedd). You can make one from the drawing shown in Fig. 131.

Fig. 132. A square pyramid similar to those made by the early Egyptians

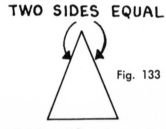

TWO SIDES EQUAL

Fig. 133

ISOSCELES TRIANGLE

Pyramids

Ask your friend what a "pyramid" is. He is almost sure to say something like, "That's what the Egyptians built." Actually a **pyramid** is a solid figure that has a flat polygon for a base, and triangular sides that meet at a point. If you look back at the tetrahedron of Fig. 112 you will see that it is a pyramid with a triangular base.

Fig. 132 shows a pyramid with a square base. It is a **regular pyramid** because it has a regular shape for the base, and the top of the pyramid is directly above the center of the base.

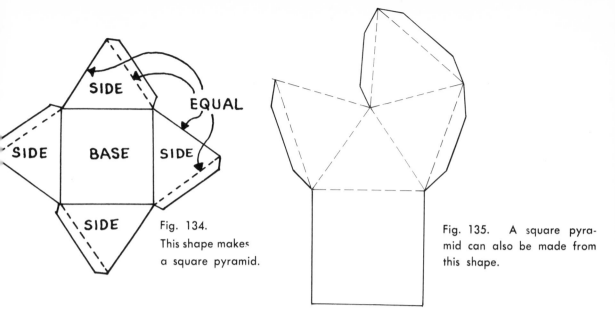

Fig. 134.
This shape makes
a square pyramid.

Fig. 135.   A square pyramid can also be made from
this shape.

Actually, a pyramid can have any polygon for a base, and the top need not be over the center.

Fig. 134 shows how to make a regular pyramid with a square base. First draw a square. On each side of the square, draw a triangle in which 2 sides are equal. Such a triangle is called **isosceles** (eye-SOSS-uh-leez, Fig. 133).

The same figure may be made in a slightly different way. Draw all the triangles touching each other, with the square base attached to one of them, as shown in Fig. 135.

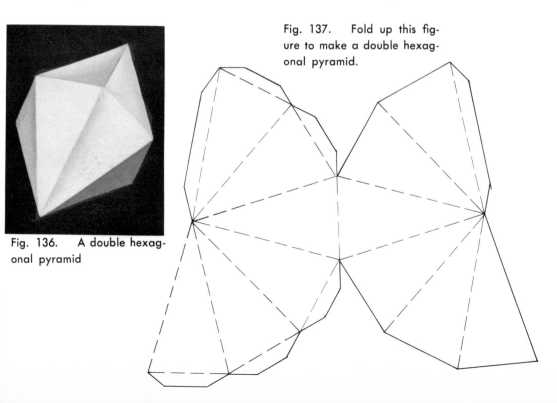

Fig. 137.   Fold up this figure to make a double hexagonal pyramid.

Fig. 136.   A double hexagonal pyramid

Many variations are possible with a pyramid shape. For example, Fig. 136 shows a **double hexagonal pyramid.** It can be made from the drawing in Fig. 137.

Fig. 138 shows another variation in which 2 hexagonal pyramids are placed on top and bottom of a hexagonal prism. This shape can be made from the drawing in Fig. 139. Note the great resemblance of this shape, to the large quartz crystal shown in Fig. 140.

Fig. 138.   This figure combines a hexagonal prism with 2 hexagonal pyramids.

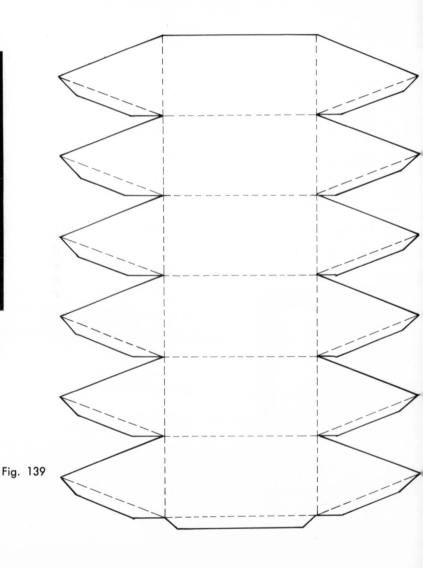

Fig. 139

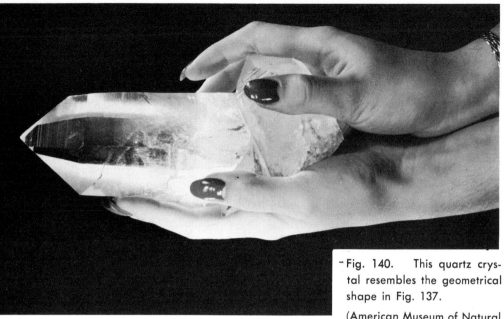

There is no limit to the changes we can make in such shapes. For example, Fig. 141 shows a solid shape that starts out as a pyramid with a pentagonal base. The triangular sides start to rise to a point. But then the top of the pyramid is cut off. Such a shape is called a **frustum of a pyramid.** We are tempted to call it a "frustrated" pyramid.

How can this figure be made? Fig. 142 shows that it starts out like a pyramid with triangular sides. A regular pentagon makes the base. Then a set of 5 **trapezoids** (Fig. 143) are formed above it. Finally, a small pentagon is tacked onto one of the trapezoids to form the top.

Cutting Corners

The shape in Fig. 144A looks somewhat familiar. It is a cube with its corners cut off. Fig. 144B shows how to make it.

A cube has 6 faces (4 sides, plus top and bottom). The same basic 6-sided shape of a cube is revealed in Fig. 144B. However, when each of the 4 corners of a side are cut off, the square is changed to an octagon. Therefore the shape in Fig. 144B has

103

6 faces that are octagons. Since a cube has 8 corners, 8 new faces are formed by cutting the corners. These faces are triangles. If the cuts are made evenly, the triangles formed at each corner will be equilateral.

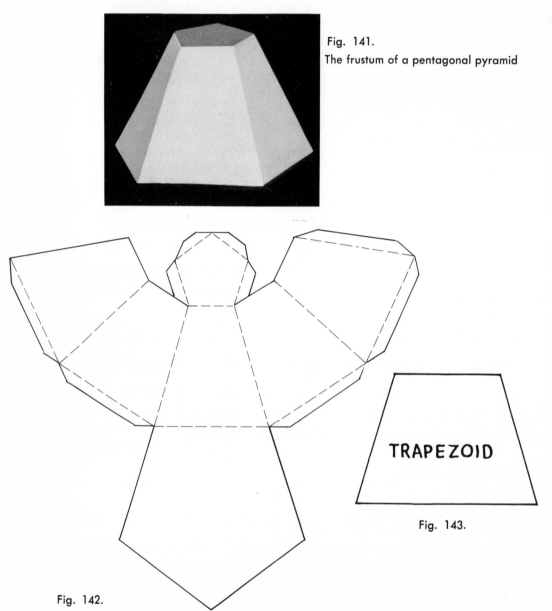

Fig. 141.
The frustum of a pentagonal pyramid

TRAPEZOID

Fig. 143.

Fig. 142.
Fold up this figure to make the frustum of a pentagonal pyramid.

104

Count the number of triangles in Fig. 144B. Note that there are 8 triangles that form the 8 triangular faces of the modified cube.

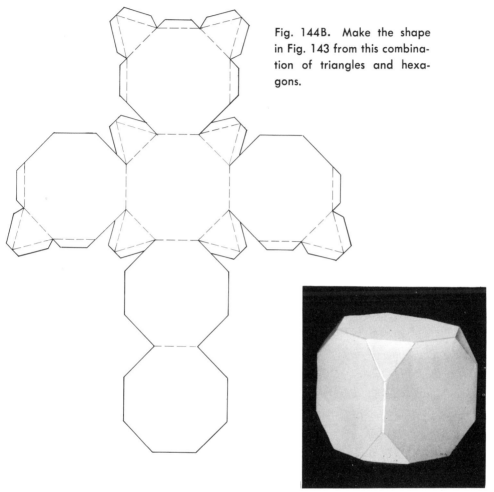

Fig. 144B. Make the shape in Fig. 143 from this combination of triangles and hexagons.

Fig. 144 A. A cube with its corners cut off

The shape shown in Fig. 145 is made from the drawing in Fig. 146. Note the resemblance of this drawing to a regular tetrahedron (Fig. 112). It starts out with the same kind of equilateral triangle arrangement. Then somehow, a hexagon formation appears.

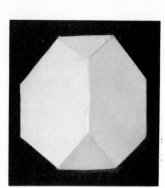

Fig. 145.   A tetrahedron
with its corners cut off

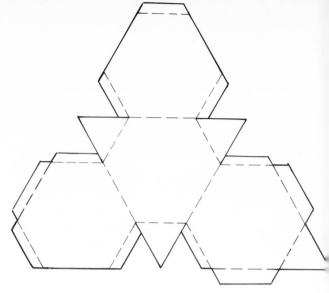

Fig. 146.   Fold up this shape to make Fig. 145.

This interesting shape is really a regular tetrahedron with its 4 corners cut off equally. As a result, the large triangular sides of the tetrahedron are changed into hexagons, and small equilateral triangles appear where the corners are cut off. To check this, note that there are 4 hexagons in Fig. 146 to correspond with the 4 equilateral triangles of the tetrahedron (Fig. 112). Then there are 4 new triangular faces for the 4 corners that are cut off. Unless the solid shape in Fig. 145 is studied carefully, one is likely to miss its basic resemblance to the tetrahedron.

The shape in Fig. 147 is made from the drawing in Fig. 148. Which shape, of those we have already considered, does this one resemble? At first, it is rather difficult to see any resemblance at all. But with practice and study of the drawing from which the shape is made, you can find the answer.

You probably do not recognize it as a modified octahedron. But look back at Fig. 116 and Fig. 117. Note that an octahedron has 8 triangular faces and 6 corners. If we cut off a small pyramid from a corner, and the shapes and the cuts are regular, squares are formed at each cut-off corner. And 6 such squares are formed from the 6 corners of the octahedron.

Fig. 147.

An octahedron with its corners cut off

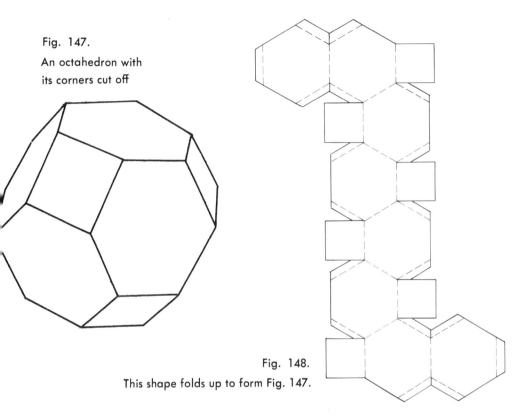

Fig. 148.
This shape folds up to form Fig. 147.

Note, too, that when each corner is cut, the triangular face is changed into an hexagonal face. Therefore, we get 8 hexagonal faces from the 8 triangular ones. Now, if you look at Fig. 148 you can see the 8 hexagons and 6 squares. The folded-up figure made from this drawing is therefore an octahedron with its corners cut off. Make it from the drawing.

A similar puzzle is presented in Fig. 149. What is it? Examine Fig. 150, from which this solid is made. First note that there is some resemblance between Fig. 150 and Fig. 148 in that both have 6 squares. But Fig. 150 differs somewhat from Fig. 148 in that the 8 hexagons are replaced by 8 triangles. That's our clue. The 6 large squares are the same 6 cut-off corners of our octahedron. But the slices are larger. In fact such a large part has been cut off that the slices meet at the centers of each edge. Each hexagon therefore shrinks to a triangle, while the squares are enlarged, as shown in Fig. 151.

Fig. 149.   An octahedron with corners cut off completely.

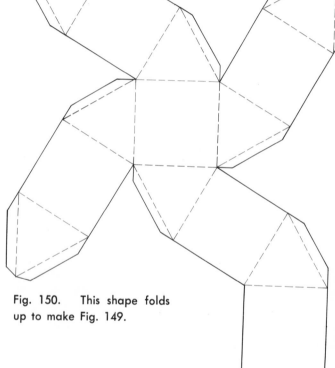

Fig. 150.   This shape folds up to make Fig. 149.

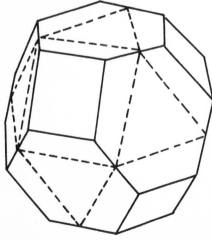

Fig. 151.   When larger pieces are cut from the corners of an octahedron, the shape becomes the one shown by the dotted lines.

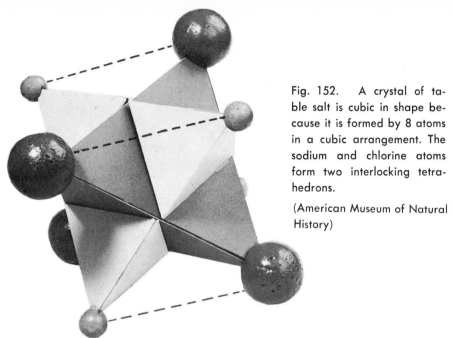

You can go on and on creating new shapes forever. Start with any simple figure. Cut off its corners in any way you please. Tack on prisms, pyramids, tetrahedrons and whatnot. Try a few shapes and see how clever you can be at designing new ones. Some may be monstrosities. But others may be very pleasing, and worth putting on exhibition.

A Variety of Shapes

Now try your hand at making the form shown in Fig. 152. It is a model of the atomic arrangement of the sodium and chlorine atoms inside ordinary table salt. One type of atom is represented by the dark spheres and the other by the small light spheres. First note that the 4 atoms of each kind form the corners of a regular tetrahedron. We can picture the 2 tetrahedrons interlocking as shown in the figure. However, if you think of the 8 atoms, disregarding their types, they form the corners of a cube, shown by the dotted lines. This cubic form is the actual crystal shape of sodium chloride, or table salt.

How would you make the solid shown in Fig. 152? We'll make several suggestions to help you.

You can begin with a series of equilateral triangles. Fold them up, one at a time to make the required shape. Discard triangles as they prove unnecessary. When you are finished unfold the figure and see what kind of flat drawing you need.

Or, better than that, figure out in advance what kind of flat drawing is needed and then fold it up to make the solid.

Note from Fig. 152 that 8 tetrahedrons are formed. You do not need bases for the tetrahedrons because all of them face the inside of the figure. Therefore, make only 3 triangles for each tetrahedron. This means 8 x 3 or 24 equilateral triangles are required. You can simplify the construction by designing one half or one fourth of the figure at a time and then tacking on the other parts. Numbering or coloring the triangles to show which tetrahedrons they form will also be of help.

This is one problem which we do not propose to solve for you. Do it yourself and get the real satisfaction of taking an important step toward mastering the subject of mathematics.

Up to this point we have dealt mainly with a branch of mathematics called **geometry,** in which shapes and forms are studied. In solving practical problems with shapes, it is necessary to combine geometry with another branch of mathematics called **algebra.** In the next chapter you will learn more about this important subject.

6

Arithmetic, Algebra and Geometry

Anybody who works with his mind can use mathematics as a basic tool. This is obviously true of engineers, scientists, and accountants. But it is also true of lawyers, doctors, salesmen, teachers, detectives, and people in general. To show the great power of mathematics, let's use it to solve a problem that seems impossibly difficult.

1. **What is the approximate weight of the air on earth?**

This may look like a puzzle that has no answer. But with some mathematics it is not difficult to solve.

You are probably familiar with a mercury barometer. This device (Fig. 153) is used to measure **air pressure.** Mercury is a very heavy liquid. It is placed in a curved tube that has no air in it (a vacuum) at the closed top (A in Fig. 153). The shorter end (B in Fig. 153) is open to the air.

It would seem that the mercury would spill out of the open end. But it doesn't. Air presses in at the open end of the tube and pushes the mercury up into the other side of the tube. If the pressure of the air is less, it doesn't push so hard and the level of the mercury drops. That's how the barometer is used to measure the air pressure.

Fig. 153. A barometer measures air pressure.

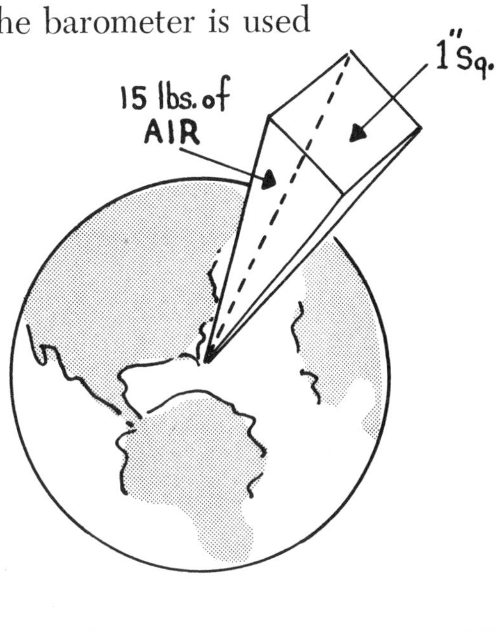

Fig. 154. The weight of air in a column 1 inch square and reaching all the way up to outer space, is 15 pounds.

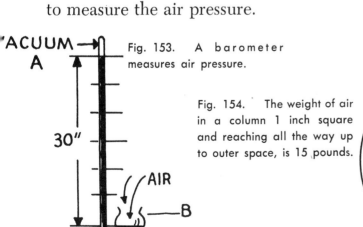

With this simple device, scientists have found that the air pressure is about 15 pounds per square inch on the surface of the earth.

What causes air pressure? The air above us has weight. When the barometer shows a pressure of 15 pounds per square inch it means that all of the air in a column 1 inch thick (1 square inch) all the way up to outer space, weighs 15 pounds (Fig. 154).

If we know how many square inches there are on the earth's surface, we can easily figure out the total weight of all the air on earth by simple multiplication. But we need not measure the number of square inches on the earth. We can calculate it from a formula. The only fact we must know is the diameter (D) of the earth.

Mathematicians give us this formula for the area of a sphere:
$$A = \pi \times D^2$$

If you are not familiar with this formula, it may look like nonsense. Yet, if you know something about the language of algebra, it is easy to use.

In the formula above, A stands for "area." The symbol π is the Greek letter "pi" (pronounced like pie). This letter stands for how many times longer the outside (circumference) of a circle is, than its diameter.

The distance around the outside (circumference) of any circle is about $3\,\frac{1}{7}$ times longer than the diameter. If we need greater accuracy, we can use the number 3.14159. If this is not accurate enough, we can carry it out to additional decimal places as follows:

3.141 592 653 589 793 238 462 643 383 279 502 88 . . .

Mathematicians have figured out this number to more than 700 decimal places. These decimal places can go on forever, because π is the kind of number that is impossible to express with a definite number of digits. For most purposes 3 1/7 (or 22/7) is close enough. Sometimes, for a rough approximation, the number 3 is sufficient.

"D" represents the diameter of the sphere. D^2 means that D is to be multiplied by itself (D x D). Read D^2 as "D squared."

We use the name "squared" because to find the area (surface) of a square we must multiply one side of the square by itself. For example, the area of a square 3 inches long on each side is 3 x 3 or 9 square inches.

What would D^3 mean? It means D multiplied by itself 3 times (D x D x D). We speak of it as "D cubed" because we get the volume (space occupied by) of a cube by multiplying its side by itself 3 times.

Now let's go to work with our formula.

$$A = \pi \times D^2$$

Because D^2 means D x D, we can also write our formula as:

$$A = \pi \times D \times D$$

You know that the diameter of the earth is 8,000 miles in length. Shall we put the number 8,000 in place of D and multiply to find the area of the earth? Yes, but we must be careful about one thing. If we use 8,000 **miles** for D, the answer will come out in **square miles.** We want the area in **square inches.** We must therefore change the 8,000 miles into feet and then into inches. We know that there are 5,280 feet to a mile and 12 inches to a foot. So we multiply 8,000 by 5,280 and then by 12 to find the number of inches in 8,000 miles.

Let's put all our information into the formula.

$$A = \pi \times D \times D$$

$$= 22/7 \times (8{,}000 \times 5{,}280 \times 12) \times (8{,}000 \times 5{,}280 \times 12) \text{ square}$$

inches.

When this multiplication is carried out we will have the number of square inches on the surface of the earth! This number must then be multiplied by 15 pounds per square inch to get the weight of all the air on earth. It is a good idea to put all numbers into place before any multiplying is done. So, we get:

Weight of air on earth (in pounds) =

$$15 \times 22/7 \times (8{,}000 \times 5{,}280 \times 12) \times (8{,}000 \times 5{,}280 \times 12).$$

Here is an important mathematical rule to remember at this point: when you have several numbers to multiply, it makes no difference in the answer which numbers you multiply first. Any order will do. For example, 2 x 3 x 4 is 24, just the same as 4 x 2 x 3 equals 24.

We may, therefore, arrange the numbers in our big multiplication in any order we like. Let's save some work by choosing a better order for the numbers.

We may multiply the numbers exactly, if we wish. But it will be quite a job. So, we'll **approximate** and get an answer that is close to the actual multiplication. We do this by rounding off the numbers. Thus we can approximate 22/7 by using 3. The number 5,280 may be approximated by using 5,000.

We get:

Weight of air on earth (in pounds) =

$$15 \times 3 \times (8{,}000 \times 5{,}000 \times 12) \times (8{,}000 \times 5{,}000 \times 12) \text{ lbs.}$$

Now, we pick easy combinations of numbers for multiplying. To avoid carrying along a lot of zeros when we multiply, we shift them all into one number at the right. Remember that when we cross off a zero at the end of one whole number, we must make up for it by attaching it to the end of another whole number. When we cross off a zero, we divide by 10. When we attach a zero to the end of another number, we multiply by 10. The net result of doing both in a multiplication (crossing off a zero in one place, and attaching one elsewhere) gives us the same answer. If there is no number to which the zero is to be attached, we start with the number 1 and attach zeros to that.

Weight of air (in pounds) =

15 x 3 x (8,000 x 5,000 x 12) x (8,000 x 5,000 x 12)

Crossing off the 12 zeros and tacking them on at the end gives us

= (15 x 3) x (8 x 5 x 12) x (8 x 5 x 12) x 1,000,000,000,000

Multiplying:

= (45) x (480) x (480) x 1,000,000,000,000 lbs.

Now we can get an approximate answer by lowering 45 to 40 and raising 480 to 500.

Weight of air = 40 x 500 x 500 x 1,000,000,000,000
= (4 x 5 x 5) x 100,000,000,000,000,000
= 100 x 100,000,000,000,000,000
= 10,000,000,000,000,000,000 lbs

This is a very clumsy number. A mathematician would simplify it by writing 10^{19}. The complete reason for the choice of 10 in this number takes us into mathematics beyond the level of this book. You can think of 10^{19} as meaning "tack on 19 zeros to the number 1."

Large numbers are read as follows:

1,000 . . . . . one thousand

1,000,000 . . . . . one million

1,000,000,000 . . . . . one billion (but not in England, where a billion is equal to our trillion).

1,000,000,000,000 . . . . . one trillion

1,000,000,000,000,000 . . . . . one quadrillion

1,000,000,000,000,000,000 . . . . . one quintillion

So, the weight of the air on earth is about 10 quintillion pounds. Or, if you prefer, the weight of the air is 10^{19} pounds. This expression is read as "ten to the nineteenth" pounds.

You may argue that this number is not exact because we raised some numbers and lowered others. You are right. But it makes little difference in the final result because the numbers we used were approximate, too.

The earth's diameter is not exactly 8,000 miles. The earth is not a perfect sphere. It is 27 miles less in diameter through the poles than through the equator.

The number 15 is not exact for air pressure. It is closer to 14.7 pounds per square inch at sea level. The pressure changes from day to day and is different all over the earth. On mountain tops the pressure drops greatly.

So, if our original figures are approximate our final answer must also be approximate, no matter how accurately we may multiply the numbers. However, scientists do this type of approximating quite often when they have to make complicated calculations with numbers that are not exact to start with.

At any rate, we have a pretty good idea about the weight of the air on earth, which we didn't have before.

How did we get this answer? We used certain kinds of knowledge.

We had to know:

Geometry—the mathematics of shapes. Knowledge in this field gave us the formula for the area of the outside surface of a sphere.

Algebra—this kind of mathematics tells us how to handle a formula properly to get the right answers.

Arithmetic—knowledge of numbers and how to work with them. This kind of mathematics enables us to calculate the answer when numbers are put into the formula.

Measurement—we needed this information to change miles into feet and then into inches.

Physics—the science of forces, motion and energy. We needed this knowledge to use the barometer and measure the air pressure.

Common sense and **Logic**—we needed these abilities to know when to combine numbers, how to make approximations, and how to juggle the numbers for ease in multiplication.

Do you see why we call mathematics a basic **tool?** Could you ever dream of weighing the air on the earth without it? Yet with this wonderful kind of knowledge you can sit down at a desk, and solve such a problem in a few minutes!

2. Mathematics in an Airplane

Many a young person dreams of becoming an airplane pilot. He pictures himself in the cockpit, pushing the stick as the airplane zooms and loops through the sky. While he dreams about airplanes, his teacher tries to give him the math he needs to become a pilot. Does he know he will have to be quite expert in mathematics to pass a pilot's exam?

Here is a typical situation in which a pilot must use math. He is flying from one city to another, 400 miles north. The speed of the airplane is 100 miles an hour. An east wind (from the east) is blowing at a speed of 25 miles an hour. In what direction should the pilot fly to arrive at his destination?

Now this is a very important problem and the pilot must solve it correctly. Even a slight mistake would take him miles off course, and that could lead to a crash.

What happens if our pilot forgets about the wind and sets his airplane straight north?

For every 100 miles the airplane flies north, the wind blows it 25 miles to the west (Fig. 155). The pilot must make up for the distance he is blown off course. He must point his airplane somewhat to the east. But how much? At what angle to the north? In which direction?

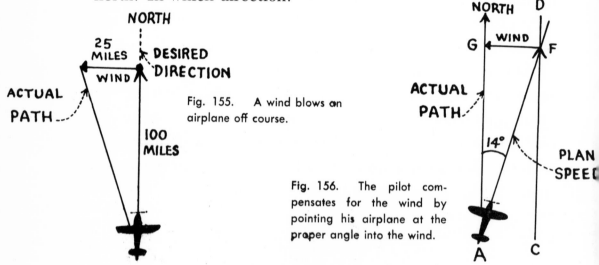

Fig. 155.   A wind blows an airplane off course.

Fig. 156.   The pilot compensates for the wind by pointing his airplane at the proper angle into the wind.

The pilot first makes a "scale" drawing (like a map). One inch on his drawing means a certain number of miles. Once the pilot selects his scale, he must use the same scale all through his calculations.

Suppose we set a scale in our drawing (Fig. 156) so that 1 inch represents 50 miles. A line 2 inches long would mean 100 miles. A line ½ inch long would mean 25 miles.

The pilot solves his problem in the following way. He draws a line (AN) straight north from A and draws another line (CD) parallel and 25 miles to the east of it (½" to the right). Then he draws a circle 2" in radius and locates the spot (F) where the circle meets the parallel line. Now, he draws the line AF. The pilot must point his airplane in the direction of the line AF and the wind will blow him back onto course. The airplane will actually travel straight north, even though it is pointing slightly east of north!

After the pilot makes this drawing (or uses his computer), he measures angle GAF with a protractor. In Fig. 156 for the particular conditions of this problem, the angle measures 14° (approximately). So the pilot points his airplane to fly 14° to the east (right) of north.

Why does the drawing give the right answer? When we draw a circle 2" in radius, we locate all the places that the airplane, starting from A and moving in any possible direction, could reach in one hour. When we draw the line CD parallel to the north line we are measuring the amount of shift caused by the wind. In one hour a balloon (without a motor) starting at the line CD will move over to line AN—blown there by the wind.

Think of the airplane's motion as having two separate parts. One part of its motion, caused by its motor and propeller, takes the airplane to F in Fig. 156 in one hour. The second part of its motion in one hour, caused by the wind, is represented by FG. Together, the two motions take the airplane to its destination at the end of the hour.

Actually the two motions do not work separately. They work together at all times to keep the airplane exactly on a north course, even though the plane is **pointing** in a different direction.

The compass indicates a different direction than the one actually being traveled, yet the plane is going north. The calculation gives the proper result when the two motions are separated, as we have done.

Before we leave our pilot, we want to point out that his problem is just beginning. Suppose the wind changes? He must change his direction or he will be off course, again. As the wind changes, he must continue to adjust his course accordingly. He will therefore have to refer frequently to his "drift indicator" and keep measuring the velocity and direction of the wind. Or, he could get local weather reports by radio.

In large airplanes a special navigator often does nothing but figure out the proper course. All sorts of things besides the wind have to be taken into account. The compass rarely points straight north. The amount it points away from north depends upon where the airplane is located on earth. The navigator must consult a map to correct the error in his compass owing to his position on earth. Then he must correct for errors caused by the magnetism of the parts of the airplane. Such errors depend upon the direction in which the airplane is pointing.

If an airplane is to take the shortest course between two cities on our globe, the pilot must change his direction frequently. It may be necessary to use a **sextant** to measure angles of the sun, moon, and stars, above the horizon. With this information, the pilot can figure out the location of his airplane on earth.

Now you can see why a would-be pilot who doesn't know mathematics had better give up the dream of piloting an airplane.

3. Building a House

Let's find out how mathematics is used in building a house. Suppose a section of a house is to be built 14 feet (14') wide with a peaked roof 4 feet (4') above the ceiling (Fig. 157). The carpenter who is building the house must buy the right size lumber and fit it together properly.

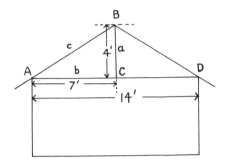

Fig. 157. The Pythagorean Theorem can be used to calculate the length of the roof beams.

If our carpenter is a poor mathematician, he might simply guess at the length of the slanted roof and order beams according to this guess. But if he buys beams that are too short, he will lose money. If he buys them too long, he will also lose money by wasting the cut-off pieces. His problem is to figure out the exact length of the slanting roof so that he can buy his lumber without waste.

Many carpenters with long experience learn the correct lengths of lumber to order. However, learning it takes many years of watching others do the job. Some carpenters make a scale drawing on paper and find the proper length that way. But a carpenter who knows his mathematics will figure it out more quickly with a bit of algebra, geometry and arithmetic. He will use the "Pythagorean (pih-THAGG-uh-REE-unn) Theorem," named after the Greek mathematician Pythagoras. It appears in many different places in mathematics, and it is used by our Einsteins as well as our carpenters.

121

Consider a "right triangle," with one of its angles a right angle (angle C in triangle ABC of Fig. 158). In such a right triangle the long side opposite the right angle is called the **hypotenuse.** Call the two short sides of the triangle (those that form the right angle), "a" and "b." Call the hypotenuse "c."

This is Pythagoras' famous theorem:

$$a^2 + b^2 = c^2$$

As we learned on page 113 this means:

$$a \text{ x } a + b \text{ x } b = c \text{ x } c$$

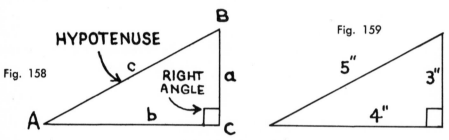

Fig. 158   HYPOTENUSE   Fig. 159

For example, the triangle in Fig. 159 has two short sides (that form the right angle) of 3″ and 4″. What is the length of the long side (hypotenuse)?

$$a^2 + b^2 \qquad = c^2$$
$$(3 \text{ x } 3) + (4 \text{ x } 4) = c \text{ x } c$$
$$9 + 16 \qquad = c \text{ x } c$$
$$25 \qquad = c \text{ x } c$$

This last line tells us that the hypotenuse multiplied by itself equals 25. What number multiplied by itself equals 25? The answer is 5; 5 times 5 equals 25. Therefore, c is 5. The long side of the triangle (the hypotenuse) in Fig. 159 is 5 inches long.

Check this for yourself. Draw a right angle and mark off the short sides of 3 inches and 4 inches. Measure the hypotenuse. If you draw the triangle carefully you will see how close to 5 inches it is. In fact it is **exactly** 5 inches.

Since a triangle with sides of 3, 4 and 5 has a right angle opposite the long side, we can make use of it to mark off right angles. Our carpenter might mark off the right angles for the corner of the house in this way: He makes a complete loop of string 12 feet long (3′+ 4′+ 5′). He puts small loops or knots at the 3′, 4′ and 5′ marks. Then the string is stretched out to form a 3-4-5 triangle using the loops or knots for the 3 corners. The angle opposite the 5′ side is a right angle.

This string method of making a right angle is much more convenient than using a bulky square. The string can be folded up and put into a pocket. Moreover the triangle can be enlarged. For example, suppose we double the former size and make the short sides of the triangle 6′ and 8′ instead of 3′ and 4′. Let's see what happens.

$$a^2 + b^2 = c^2$$
$$(6 \times 6) + (8 \times 8) = c \times c$$
$$36 + 64 = c \times c$$
$$100 = c \times c$$

What number multiplied by itself gives 100? The answer is 10. We know that c is equal to 10. Thus, a 6-8-10 triangle is also a right triangle. Notice that all the sides of this triangle are exactly double those of the 3-4-5 triangle.

Now we are ready to return to our carpenter and his problem of finding the proper length to order for his roof beams. The line BC in Fig. 157 is perpendicular to the ceiling (AD) and also divides the roof line in half. So, AC is half of 14′, or 7′. The peak of the roof is to be 4′ above the ceiling. Therefore, "a" is 4′ and "b" is 7′.

$$a^2 + b^2 \quad = c^2$$
$$(4 \times 4) + (7 \times 7) = c \times c$$
$$16 + 49 \quad = c \times c$$
$$65 \quad\quad = c \times c$$

Now, what number multiplied by itself gives 65? Is it 8 x 8? No, that gives 64. Is it 9 x 9? No, that gives 81. But the answer is somewhere between 8 and 9.

A mathematician or engineer would handle this problem by "finding the square root" of 65. This can be done in several different ways. He might use a slide rule to get a close answer in a few seconds. He might consult a table of "square roots." He might use a special table of **logarithms** which changes the problem of finding the square root into a simple one of taking half of a number. Or he might use arithmetic similar to long division to work it out.

In our carpentry problem if we get the answer to a fraction of a foot, it is close enough because lumber is sold in multiples of 2 feet. Thus, the carpenter could buy 8′ or 10′ lengths. Or he could buy 18′ lengths and cut them in half to give a 9′ length. Should he use 8′ or 9′ pieces? The length of the roof beam being slightly more than 8′, an 8′ beam would be too short, since some of the length must be cut off to make the angles. A 9′ length would be a good length to use. Therefore, our mathematical carpenter buys the 18′ lengths and cuts them to size.

Suppose we want to find the length of the beams more accurately. One easy way is to try multiplying numbers at intervals of a tenth of a foot. In our problem above we want to find a number that equals 65 when multiplied by itself. Let's try 8.1. We find that 8.1 x 8.1 equals 65.61. We are a fraction too high. But it so close that for our purposes we can say the answer is 8.1′. This is just slightly more than 8 feet and 1 inch.

It should be clear from this that anyone who plans to do any carpentry will find mathematics a most useful tool.

4. Speed of Earth in Space

Let us now take an example of the use of mathematics in astronomy. You have learned in school that the speed of the earth around the sun is about 18 miles a second. How is it figured out?

It's just a few minutes work, once the distance to the sun is known. We know that the distance to the sun is approximately 93,000,000 miles.

Fig. 160 shows the almost circular path of the earth as it revolves about the sun. The radius of the circle is approximately 93,000,000 miles, the average distance of the earth from the sun.

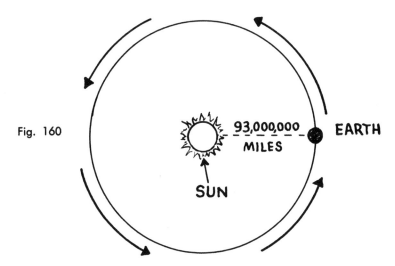

Fig. 160

To obtain the speed of any moving object, we should know the distance traveled in a certain time. That is, the distance must be divided by the time it takes to travel.

$$\text{Speed} = \frac{\text{distance}}{\text{time}}$$

For example, what is the speed of an automobile that travels 80 miles in 2 hours?

$$\text{Speed} = \frac{\text{distance}}{\text{time}} = \frac{80 \text{ miles}}{2 \text{ hours}} = 40 \text{ miles an hour}$$

What is the speed of the earth as it travels around the sun? Let's take one year as the period of time. The distance is one complete revolution around the sun, the "circumference" of the almost circular orbit of the earth.

Mathematicians tell us that the circumference (C) of a circle is given by this formula:

$$C = 2 \pi r$$
$$\text{or, } C = 2 \times \pi \times r$$

In this formula C is the circumference; π (pi) is the number 3-1/7 (or 22/7), and r is the radius of the circle. The circumference of the orbit of the earth is therefore:

$$C = 2 \times \frac{22}{7} \times 93{,}000{,}000 \text{ miles}$$

This is the distance the earth travels in miles, in a year.

Let's find the speed of the earth in miles per **second.** There are 365 days in a year, 24 hours in a day, 60 minutes in an hour, and 60 seconds in a minute. Therefore, there are 365 x 24 x 60 x 60 seconds in a year.

The speed of the earth is then:

$$\text{Speed} = \frac{\text{distance}}{\text{time}}$$

$$= \frac{2 \times 22/7 \times 93{,}000{,}000}{365 \times 24 \times 60 \times 60} \text{ miles per second.}$$

You can figure this out exactly, if you wish. But let us first approximate by changing 22/7 to 3; 93,000,000 to 100,000,000; and also change 365 to 400; and 24 to 25. We get:

$$\text{Speed} = \frac{2 \times 3 \times 100{,}000{,}000}{400 \times 25 \times 60 \times 60}$$

Cross out zeros in the numerator and compensate by crossing out an equal number of zeros in the denominator.

$$\text{Speed} = \frac{2 \times 3 \times 10{,}000}{4 \times 25 \times 6 \times 6}$$

Now, 2 x 3 is 6, which can be divided into 6 in the denominator to give 1. Also 4 x 25 gives 100. So,

$$\text{Speed} = \frac{10{,}000}{100 \times 6}$$

Now cross out 2 zeros in the numerator and also in the denominator. And divide 6 into 100. We get

Speed = 17 miles per second (approx.)

This is quite close to the figure of 18 miles per second. Try to get the answer exactly by using the original numbers, instead of approximating.

5. Speed of an Earth Satellite

You read in the papers that an earth satellite needs a speed of at least 5 miles a second to stay in orbit. Scientists figured this out by using mathematical formulas. To show the power of mathematical formulas, we are going to use a formula to figure out the speed needed by an earth satellite.

If the earth satellite travels around the earth in a circular orbit, and not too far out in space, then the approximate speed is given by this formula:

$S^2 = 32 \times R$ (feet per second)

S is the speed of the earth satellite in feet per second. S^2 means S x S, and R stands for the radius of the earth in feet. In this book we cannot explain how this formula is obtained. We'll leave that for you to find out, when you learn more about physics and mathematics.

We know that the diameter of the earth is 8,000 miles. The distance to the center (radius) of the earth is therefore 4,000 miles. We change the miles to feet by multiplying by 5,280.

$$S^2 = 32 \times R \text{ (feet per second)}$$
$$= 32 \times 4{,}000 \times 5{,}280$$
$$= 676{,}000{,}000 \text{ (approx.)}$$

Now we have to find the number which, when multiplied by itself, gives 676,000,000. We call this number the "square root" of 676,000,000.

Let's try 10,000 x 10,000. We get 100,000,000. It's too small. We try 20,000 x 20,000 and get 400,000,000. If we try 30,000 x 30,000, we get 900,000,000. This is too high. The number we seek is therefore somewhere between 20,000 and 30,000. With 25,000 x 25,000, we get 625,000,000. Multiplying 26,000 x 26,000, we get 676,000,000. We are close enough. The number, which when multiplied by itself equals 676,000,000 is 26,000.

The speed needed by an earth satellite is thus about 26,000 feet per second.

We are accustomed to speeds expressed in miles rather than in feet. We therefore divide 26,000 by 5,280. We get approximately 5 miles a second. That's the speed needed by an earth satellite in order to stay in an orbit above the earth's surface. Mathematics is certainly a powerful tool if it can obtain such results!

6. Center of Gravity

If you watch an airplane being loaded with cargo, you will see that each piece is weighed before it is placed on board the ship. A man with a special slide rule observes the weight of the package and makes a calculation. He then instructs the freight handlers where to put the parcel in the airplane.

This man is measuring the effect of the weight on the center of gravity (or balance point) of the airplane. If too much weight is put up front, it makes the airplane "nose-heavy" and the pilot will have to keep fighting the plane's tendency to nose downward. On the other hand, if too much cargo is put into the back of the airplane, it becomes "tail-heavy" and the pilot will have to worry about its tendency to keep nosing up into a stall. If too much weight is placed to one side, the airplane will constantly tend to bank (dip its wing).

You can do a few simple experiments to get some idea of the way mathematics can be used to figure out the positions of centers of gravity.

Cut out any triangle from a piece of cardboard. Try to balance it on a pencil point (Fig. 161). You may succeed by trial and error. However, there is a simple way to find the balance point in advance.

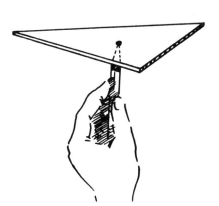

Fig. 161. A cardboard triangle will balance on a pencil point if supported at the center of gravity.

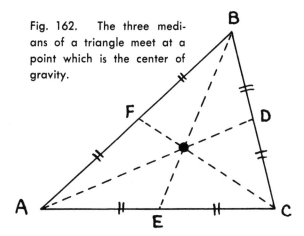

Fig. 162. The three medians of a triangle meet at a point which is the center of gravity.

Fig. 162 shows the triangle ABC. Locate the midpoints of each side of the triangle (D, E, and F). Draw a line from each corner to the midpoint of its opposite side (AD, BE and CF). These lines are called **medians.** They meet at a certain point which is the **center of gravity** of the triangle. The triangle balances when it is supported at this point. Try it.

Now let's consider a different kind of center of gravity problem, one in which two weights are on a horizontal stick. This is closer to the airplane situation than is our triangle problem. Fig. 163 shows one weight of 5 lbs. and another of 1 lb., 12 inches apart on a stick. Assume that the stick is very light and its weight does not have to be taken into account. At what point on the stick will this device balance perfectly, if suspended by a string?

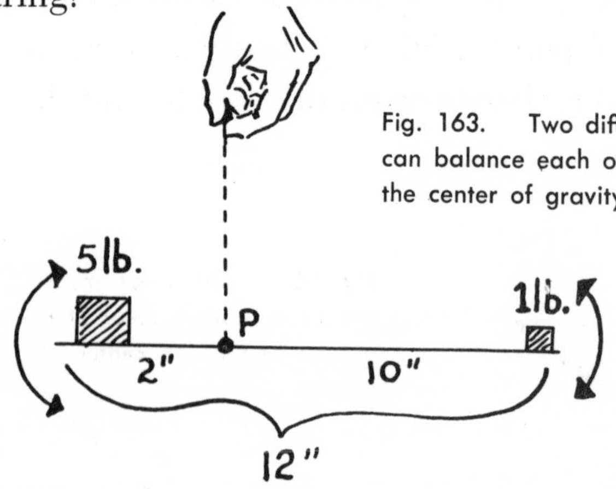

Fig. 163.   Two different weights on a bar can balance each other when supported at the center of gravity.

Each weight on a stick has "leverage." The point (P in Fig. 163) around which the bar turns is called the **fulcrum,** or pivot. The further away from the fulcrum, the greater the effect of a weight in turning a bar. In other words if you have a crowbar with a long handle, a small effort on the far end can be made to have a large effect, depending upon where you put the fulcrum.

It has been found that we can make up for the smaller weight by placing it farther away from the pivot, so that a weight of 1 lb. can balance a weight of 5 lbs. If we place the 1 lb. weight 5 times farther away from the fulcrum (pivot) than the 5 lb. weight, then the two will balance.

Look at Fig. 163. You see that the pivot is placed 2″ from the 5 lb. weight and 10″ from the 1 lb. weight. It means that the 1 lb. weight is 5 times as far from the pivot as the 5 lb. weight. If suspended at this point, the bar will balance perfectly. We have found its center of gravity.

This kind of calculation, with formulas, must be performed with every large parcel that is placed into a large airplane!

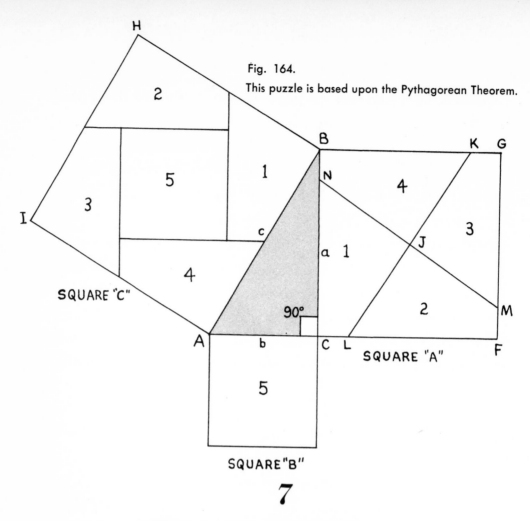

Fig. 164.

This puzzle is based upon the Pythagorean Theorem.

7

Mathematical Games and Puzzles

1. The Pythagorean Theorem, as described on page 121 is the basis for an interesting puzzle.

Draw any right triangle (ABC in Fig. 164) with AB as hypotenuse (long side) and angle C equal to 90°. Now draw a square (BCFG) on side BC. Draw another square (ACDE) on AC. Draw a third square (ABHI) on AB.

If the square on "a" and the square on "b" are cut apart properly, they can be put together to form the larger square on "c." This comes from the fact that in a right triangle:

$$a^2 + b^2 = c^2$$

(a squared) + (b squared) = (c squared)

Since a² is (a x a), it is also equal to the area of the square based on "a." In the same way, b² is the area of the square based .on "b," and c² is the area of the square based on "c." Thus, the expression a² + b² = c² tells us that the area of "square a" plus the area of "square b" should equal the area of "square c."

Now, it should be possible to cut apart the squares on "a" and "b" and fit them together to form the square on "c." You can do this as follows: Start by finding the center (J) of the medium-sized "square a." This is easily done by drawing the 2 diagonals, BF and CG. They meet at J. Draw a line (KL), through J, parallel to the hypotenuse AB. Draw a line (MN), perpendicular to KL, through J. These 2 lines cut the square into 4 equal parts (1, 2, 3, and 4). When put together with the small square (5), all the pieces fit perfectly into the big square "c," as shown in Fig. 164.

Make the puzzle, as shown, drawing the 3 squares and the triangle on thin cardboard. On another piece of cardboard, draw the squares based on "a" and "b." Cut the square on "a" apart on the lines KL and MN. Show a friend that the 4 pieces fit into the square BGFC and that the small uncut square fits on ACDE. Then challenge him to fit the 5 pieces together into the large square. It is quite difficult to do.

If you want to make the puzzle more difficult, cut square ACDE into several parts in any way you wish. The parts are extremely difficult to assemble, if you do not know the trick.

2. Secret

We call this game Secret because the one who knows the mathematical secret can always win.

Place 20 to 30 small objects on a table. Any kind of object

will do (pennies, washers, toothpicks, cards, etc.). The exact number of objects does not matter.

The game is played by 2 people. Each player must pick up one or more objects and put them aside. But in no case may a player take more than 5. The winner of the game is the one who picks up the last object. Each player tries to move in such a way that he picks up the last one.

At first, the game will seem to be a matter of luck. But there is a rule for winning the game. Let's analyze the game and find the rule.

Suppose there are 1, 2, 3, 4 or 5 objects left on the table. You can win by taking all 5 of them away. But suppose there are 6 objects left. Then you lose, because you can't move more than 5. If you take 5 your opponent can take the last object and win. On the other hand, if you take 1, 2, 3, or 4, your opponent can take the remaining objects to win the game. So if a player is faced with 6 on the table, he loses.

Suppose you are faced with 7, 8, 9, 10, or 11 objects. You can always win by taking away enough to leave your opponent 6. He will then lose.

Suppose you are faced with 12. No matter what you do, whether you take 1, 2, 3, 4 or 5, your opponent can take away enough to leave 6 and you will lose. Therefore, 12 is also a losing number for the person who must make a move.

In the same way, you can show that 18 is a loss for the person who has to move, provided the other fellow knows how to move. No matter how many objects a player removes from the 18, the other player can always take away enough to leave 12. If you leave your opponent any combination of 6's (multiples of 6), he will lose. Thus, to be sure of a win, you must move in such a way that you leave 6, 12, 18, 24, etc., for your opponent.

Let's take a sample game between 2 players. You and X. Assume that the game starts with 23 objects and X goes first. Your objective is to reach 18, 12 and then 6. X doesn't know the rule. Suppose he takes 3 from the 23 and leaves 20.

You can now take away 2, to leave 18. You have now won the game. Let's say that your opponent takes away 2 to leave 16. You take away 4 to leave 12. That's a losing number.

Suppose he now takes away 5. You take away 1 to leave 6.

Suppose he takes away 1. You now take away 5 and win.

What if the rule is changed so that no more than 4 may be taken away? Add 1 to the number (4) to get 5. Now you will win by leaving your opponent 5, 10, 15, or any other multiple of 5.

To get the winning combination, simply add 1 to the number representing the most that can be taken away, and then move in such a way as to leave multiples of that number.

3. Nim

The game of Nim is similar to Secret, but the rule for winning is more complicated.

Make 3 piles of objects, with about 6 to 10, or more, in each stack. Be sure there is a different number of objects in all three stacks. A player is allowed to take away as many objects as he pleases from any pile, even the entire pile. But he may only take objects from one pile at a time. As in the game of Secret, the player who picks up the last object is the winner.

A simple rule for winning will work in many cases: wait until your opponent leaves the same number of objects in two of the piles. Then you take away the whole third stack leaving him with the two equal stacks. Now, whatever he does, you do the same. If he takes 1, you take 1 from the other stack. If he takes 4 from one pile, you take 4 from the other. When the 2 stacks have only 1 object each, your opponent must take away one of the objects, you take away the other and win.

In addition, if you leave your opponent with 3 stacks of 1, 2 and 3 objects, you will win, because no matter what he does, you can then always make 2 of the stacks equal. For example, if your opponent leaves you with 2, 3 and 5, take 4 to change the 5 to 1 and reach the winning combination of 1, 2, 3. Suppose your opponent leaves you with 3, 5 and 5. Take away the 3 and leave him with two equal stacks of 5.

There is a rule that will enable you to win from the very first move or two. This involves expressing numbers in what is called the "binary" (BY-nuh-ree) system instead of the decimal system.

From your earliest days in school you were taught the numbers 1, 2, 3, 4, 5, 6, 7, 8, 9, 10, etc. You may have wondered why the numbers were chosen to repeat after 10. It seems to have developed long ago from the fact that we have 10 fingers we can use to count on. If we had 12 fingers it is probable, that in addition to the numbers from 0 to 9, we would have two additional number symbols, one for "10" and another for "11." Then we would write our "12" as "10."

Let's analyze the number 10. What does it really mean? The first digit (1) tells how many tens there are. The second digit (0) tells how many units there are. So, the number 10 means "1 ten plus zero." In our **decimal** system the number 11 means "1 ten plus 1." The number 45 means "4 tens plus 5."

But, if we had a number system based upon twelves, the number we write as 23 would mean "2 twelves plus 3," and would be equal to our 27!

Mathematicians have found that a number system based upon 2 has great advantages for electronic computing machines. Such a **binary** (two digit) **system** uses only the digits 1 and 0. In certain types of electronic computers the "1" means that the current is "on" in a circuit, while the "0" means that the current is "off." A number may then be expressed with lights on a panel as shown in Fig. 165. The number shown on the panel is "1010." What does this number mean in our customary decimal system? Let's build up the numbers starting with 1.

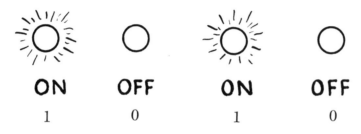

| ON | OFF | ON | OFF |
| 1 | 0 | 1 | 0 |

Fig. 165. A computer can represent numbers in the binary system by using lights that are on or off.

The first number (1) remains the same as in the regular number system. But what about 2? This number is not permitted. We must now write 2 as 10, the next higher number. Remember that this number "10" in the binary system is not our regular 10. It means "one 2, plus zero."

In the binary system our 3 would be expressed as "11." This means "one 2 plus 1." We have used "ones" in both places for our 3, expressed as "11" and we do not have another figure to use. The only digits we have are 0 and 1, the next number (our 4) must go into 3 digits. Thus our 4 is represented by "100" in the binary system. Continue in this way to build up the numbers in our decimal system and their equivalents in the binary system.

Decimal system	Binary system
1	1
2	10
3	11
4	100
5	101
6	110
7	111
8	1000
9	1001
10	1010
11	1011
12	1100
13	1101
14	1110
15	1111
16	10000

Check the correctness of this binary system by trying a few arithmetic problems. You know that 2 x 2 is 4. In the binary system, 10 stands for our 2. Thus 2 x 2 is expressed as 10 x 10 with the answer 100 in the binary system, which is 4 in our decimal system. This checks.

What is 2 x 4? In the decimal system we get 8. In the binary system we get 10 x 100 equals 1000. This checks in the table with the answer of 8.

What is 3 + 6? In the decimal system the answer is 9. How would we get the same result in the binary system? In that system 3 is represented by "11" and 6 is represented by "110."

We write the sum as follows, using the letters A, B and C to identify the columns.

$$
\begin{array}{r}
\underline{\text{ABC}} \\
11 = 3 \\
+\,110 = 6 \\
\overline{\text{?1} \quad 9}
\end{array}
$$

Adding the 1 and 0 in column C gives 1. We put it down on the bottom line. Now we run into trouble in column B, where we have 1 plus 1. We are not permitted to write "2." In the binary system 2 is "10." Therefore we put a "0" in column B and carry the 1 into column A as follows:

$$
\begin{array}{r}
\underline{\text{ABC}} \\
11 \\
+\,110 \\
\overline{\text{?01}}
\end{array}
$$

Now we have the same problem in column A. But, as before 1 + 1 add up to 2, which in the binary system is expressed as "10." Therefore:

$$
\begin{array}{r}
11 \\
+\,110 \\
\overline{1001}
\end{array}
$$

Look up the number "1001" in the table. You will see that it is 9. Thus, addition in the binary system works out the same as our system based upon tens (the decimal system).

Now let's see how to win any game of Nim.

Express the number of objects in each pile as numbers in the binary system. But, add them up in the decimal system! The total in any column will be either even or odd. If you move in such a way that all columns add up to 0 or 2, you will win.

For example, you are faced with the combination 5, 6, and 7. How should you move to win?

From the table above we see that 5 in the binary system is "101," 6 is "110," and 7 is "111." Add them up:

$$5 = 101$$
$$6 = 110$$
$$7 = \underline{111}$$
$$322$$

We must change the odd number 3 to an even number (2 or 0).

One way to do this is to change the 111 to 11. We get:

$$101$$
$$110$$
$$\underline{11}$$
$$222$$

This is a combination that wins. We arrive at it by changing 111 (7 in the decimal system) to 11 (3 in the decimal system). Therefore, a right move is to change 7 to 3. Take 4 objects from the stack with 7 objects to leave 3. There are two other moves that will leave winning combinations. See if you can find them.

Using the binary system, you can find the winning combination for any 3 numbers. If you learn some of these combinations, you can beat anyone else who doesn't know the way to win.

Now Try These

(Answers on Page 142)

1. Mr. Blake is a lawyer who conducts business in 3 different cities. Fig. 166 shows the location (A, B, C) of these cities on the map. He wants to build a house, located in such a way that it will be exactly the same distance from all 3 cities. He will then be able to drive to each city in about the same length of time. Where should he buy land for his house?

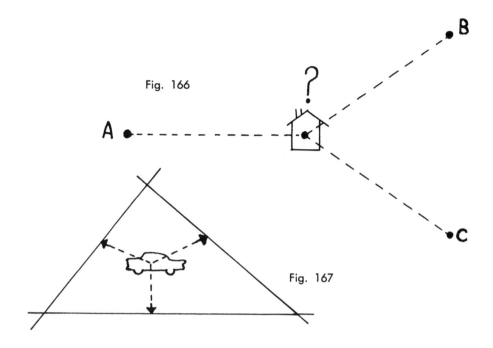

Fig. 166

Fig. 167

2. An escaped convict is fleeing in a stolen automobile. The police expect him to take one of three main roads, as shown in Fig. 167. Only one police car is available in that area at the time. Headquarters, therefore, informs Trooper Cooper to station himself somewhere in the triangle formed by the three main roads so that he can get to any road quickly, as soon as a report comes in.

Trooper Cooper is somewhat of a mathematician. In fact, he happens to have a compass with him. He makes a few arcs and lines on his map and locates the exact spot where he can be the same distance from each of the three roads. He stations himself at this point so as to have the best chance of intercepting the fleeing convict. Where does Trooper Cooper wait?

3. To save time and labor, a tunnel will be driven through the mountain from opposite ends at the same time (Fig. 168). But the engineers want to be very sure that the tunnels from each end will meet under the mountain and not pass each other. How can they do it?

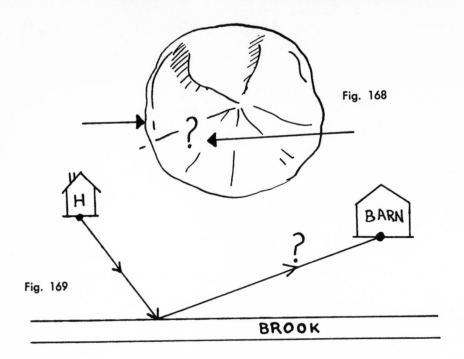

Fig. 168

Fig. 169

BROOK

4. Farmer Lang likes to take a drink of cool water from the brook each morning on his way to the barn (Fig. 169). Since he also likes to save steps, he figures out the best path to take to reduce the distance he must walk each day. How does he do it?

9

Answers to Problems

Answer to problem 1 on page 140

The problem is solved by constructing a circle that passes through the 3 cities. On a map draw lines connecting the cities (triangle ABC in Fig. 170). Draw the perpendicular bisectors of each side using the method shown on page 37. The 3 perpendicular bisectors of the sides of the triangle meet at a single point (D).

We can check to see if D is equally distant from the points A, B, and C. Adjust your compass so that its radius equals AD, and draw a circle with D as center. The circle passes right

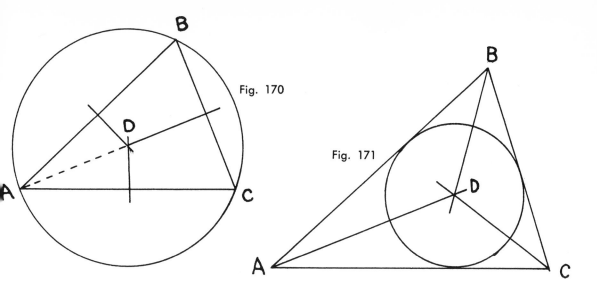

Fig. 170

Fig. 171

through the other 2 points, B and C. Since all 3 points are on the same circle they must be equally distant from the center, D.

The construction in this problem is called "circumscribing a circle about a triangle."

Answer to problem 2 on page 141

Using the method shown on page 55, draw the bisector of each angle of the triangle formed by the three roads. All 3 angle bisectors meet at a point inside the triangle (D in Fig. 171). Adjust your compass so that a circle drawn with D as center is tangent (touching) to one of the sides of the triangle (roads). You will find that the circle is also tangent to the other two roads. If Trooper Cooper stations himself at D, he is in the best position for reaching any of the three roads.

The construction in this problem is called "inscribing a circle in a triangle."

Answer to problem 3 on page 141

The engineers set the surveyors to work making the lines and angles shown in Fig. 172. The line of the tunnel is AB. An angle (ABC) is then constructed with any convenient number of degrees. Then the **same** size angle is constructed at C (angle BCD). Line CD is now parallel to AB.

A similar construction of lines is made at the other side of the mountain at D, E, and F, using equal angles. And DE is made equal to BC. If the second tunnel is driven through the mountain at G in the direction FE, it will meet the tunnel from AB.

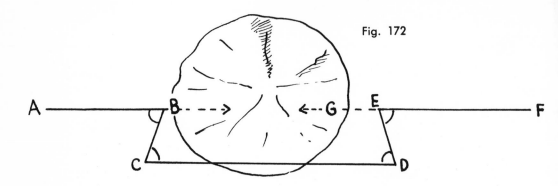

Fig. 172

Surveyors work so accurately that the tunnels dug under mountains and rivers will usually meet with an error of no more than an inch.

Answer to problem 4 on page 142

The quickest and shortest route is the path a ray of light would take in bouncing off a mirror placed along the line of the brook. Draw a map of the house, brook, and barn (Fig. 173). On the map, drop a perpendicular from the house to the line of the brook, and extend it an equal distance, to B. Now draw a straight line from B to the barn. It crosses the brook at C. If Farmer Lang heads for C, he takes the shortest distance to the brook and then to the barn.

Incidentally, if you measure angles 1 and 2 in Fig. 173 you will find they are equal. This is exactly the way a beam of light hits a mirror. It bounces off an object at the same angle as the

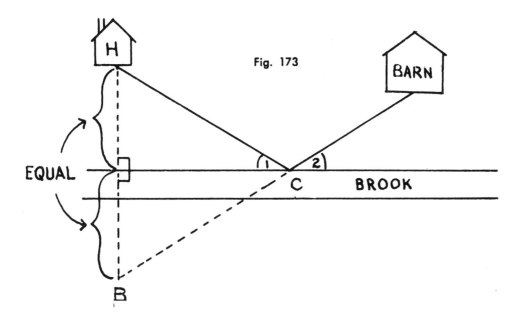

Fig. 173

angle at which it strikes. In other words, a beam of light reaches a spot after reflecting from a mirror, by taking the shortest possible path—like Farmer Lang. This fact is important in the theory of light.

Now, you have reached the last page of this book. But it is just a beginning for further exploration. In this book you touched the surface of the great subject of mathematics and gained a general appreciation of its value in our modern world.

The more you learn about mathematics, the more will you realize the wonders it contains, and the greater will be your understanding of nature, of industry, of yourself and the world of the future.

Perhaps you have begun to see that mathematics need not be dull work. It can be as interesting and stimulating as you wish to make it.

9

Books About Mathematics

Fun with Mathematics
    Jerome S. Meyer
    (World Publishing)

Fun with Figures
    Mae and Ira Freeman
    (Random House)

The Wonderful World of
    Mathematics
    Lancelot Hogben
    (Garden City Books)

Mathematical Puzzles for Be-
    ginners and Enthusiasts
    Geoffrey Mott-Smith
    (Dover)

Mathematics Magic and
    Mystery
    Martin Gardner
    (Dover)

An Adventure in Geometry
    Anthony Ravielli
    (Viking)

10

Pronouncing Index